Happ[illegible]

T[illegible]

Happy & wishing the best Easter Ever!

April, 2023 Dr. Olga

A JOURNEY OF RICHES

Master Your Mindset

11 Inspiring insights for creating a fulfilling life

A Journey Of Riches – Master Your Mindset

11 Inspiring insights for creating a fulfilling life

Published by Motion Media International
Editors: Kit Brookman, Daniel Decillis, Eric Wyman, Yasmin Phillip, and Katie Beck.
Cover Design: Motion Media International
Typesetting & Assembly: Motion Media International

Printing: Amazon
Creator: John Spender - Primary Author
Title: *A Journey of Riches – Master Your Mindset*
ISBN Digital: 978-1-925919-55-4
ISBN Print: 978-1-925919-56-1
Subjects: Motivation, Inspiration

Praise For *A Journey of Riches* Book Series

"The *A Journey of Riches* book series is a great collection of inspiring short stories that will leave you wanting more!"
~ Alex Hoffmann, Network Marketing Guru.

"If you are looking for an inspiring read to get you through any change, this is it! This book is comprised of many gripping perspectives from a collection of successful international authors with a tone of wisdom to share."
~ Theera Phetmalaigul, Entrepreneur/Investor.

"*A Journey of Riches* is an empowering series that implements two simple words in overcoming life's struggles.

By diving into the meaning of the words 'problem' and 'challenge,' you will find yourself motivated to believe in the triumph of perseverance. With many different authors from all around the world coming together to share various stories of life's trials, you will find yourself drenched in encouragement to push through even the darkest of battles. The stories are heartfelt personal shares of moving through and transforming challenges into rich life experiences.

The book will move, touch, and inspire your spirit to face and overcome any of life's adversities. It is a truly inspirational read. Thank you for being the kind, open soul you are, John!"
~ Casey Plouffe, Seven Figure Network Marketer.

"A must-read for anyone facing major changes or challenges in life right now. This book will give you the courage to move through any struggle with confidence, grace, and ease."
~ Jo-Anne Irwin, Transformational Coach and Best-Selling Author.

"I have enjoyed the *Journey of Riches* book series. Each person's story is written from the heart, and everyone's journey is different. We all have a story to tell, and John Spender does an amazing job of finding authors and combining their stories into uplifting books."
~ Liz Misner Palmer, Foreign Service Officer.

"A timely read as I'm facing a few challenges right now. I like the various insights from the different authors. This book will inspire you to move through any challenge or change that you are experiencing."
~ David Ostrand, Business Owner.

"I've known John Spender for a while now, and I was blessed with an opportunity to be in book four in the series. I know that you will enjoy this new journey, like the rest of the books in the series. The collection of stories will assist you with making changes, dealing with challenges, and seeing that transformation is possible for your life."
~ Charlie O' Shea, Entrepreneur.

"*A Journey of Riches* series will draw you in and help you dig deep into your soul. These authors have unbelievable life stories of purpose inside of them. John Spender is dedicated to bringing peace, love, and adventure to the world of his readers! Dive into this series, and you will be transformed!"
~ Jeana Matichak, Author of *Finding Peace*.

"Awesome! Truly inspirational! It is amazing what the human spirit can achieve and overcome! Highly recommended!"
~ Fabrice Beliard, Australian Business Coach and Best-Selling Author.

"*A Journey of Riches* Series is a must-read. It is an empowering collection of inspirational and moving stories, full of courage, strength, and heart. Bringing peace and awareness to those lucky enough to read to assist and inspire them on their life journey."
~ Gemma Castiglia, Avalon Healing, Best Selling Author.

"The *A Journey of Riches* book series is an inspirational collection of books that will empower you to take on any challenge or change in life."
~ Kay Newton, Midlife Stress Buster, and Best-Selling Author.

"*A Journey of Riches* book series is an inspiring collection of stories, sharing many different ideas and perspectives on how to overcome challenges, deal with change and make empowering choices in your life. Open the book anywhere and let your mood choose where you need to read. Buy one of the books today; you'll be glad that you did!"
~ Trish Rock, Modern Day Intuitive, Best-Selling Author, Speaker, Psychic & Holistic Coach.

"*A Journey of Riches* is another inspiring read. The authors are from all over the world, and each has a unique perspective to share that will have you thinking differently about your current circumstances in life. An insightful read!"
~ Alexandria Calamel, Success Coach and Best-Selling Author.

"The *A Journey of Riches* book series is a collection of real-life stories, which are truly inspiring and give you the confidence that no matter what you are dealing with in your life, there is a light at the end of the tunnel, and a very bright one at that. Totally empowering!"
~ John Abbott, Freedom Entrepreneur.

"An amazing collection of true stories from individuals who have overcome great changes, and who have transformed their lives and used their experience to uplift, inspire and support others."
~ Carol Williams, Author, Speaker & Coach.

"You can empower yourself from the power within this book that can help awaken the sleeping giant within you. John has a purpose in life to bring inspiring people together to share their wisdom for the benefit of all who venture deep into this book series. If you are looking for inspiration to be someone special, this book can be your guide."
~ Bill Bilwani, Renowned Melbourne Restaurateur.

"In the *A Journey of Riches* series, you will catch the impulse to step up, reconsider and settle for only the very best for yourself and those around you. Penned from the heart and with an unflinching drive to make a difference for the good of all, *A Journey of Riches* series is a must-read."
~ Steve Coleman, author of *Decisions, Decisions! How to Make the Right One Every Time.*

"Do you want to be on top of your game? *A Journey of Riches* is a must-read with breakthrough insights that will help you do just that!"
~ Christopher Chen, Entrepreneur.

"In *A Journey of Riches*, you will find the insight, resources, and tools you need to transform your life. By reading the author's stories, you, too, can be inspired to achieve your greatest accomplishments and what is truly possible for you. Reading this book activates your true potential for transforming your life way beyond what you think is possible. Read it and learn how you, too, can have a magical life."
~ Elaine Mc Guinness, Best Selling Author of *Unleash Your Authentic Self!*

"If you are looking for an inspiring read, look no further than the *A Journey of Riches* book series. The books are an inspiring collection of short stories that will encourage you to embrace life even more. I highly recommend you read one of the books today!"
~ Kara Dono, Doula, Healer, and Best-Selling Author.

"*A Journey of Riches* series is a must-read for anyone seeking to enrich their own lives and gain wisdom through the wonderful stories of personal empowerment & triumphs over life's challenges. I've given several copies to my family, friends, and clients to inspire and support them to step into their greatness. I highly recommend that you read these books, savoring the many 'aha's' and tools you will discover inside."
~ Michele Cempaka, Hypnotherapist, Shaman, Transformational Coach & Reiki Master.

"If you are looking for an inspirational read, look no further than the *A Journey of Riches* book series. The books are an inspiring and educational collection of short stories from the author's soul that will encourage you to embrace life even more. I've even given them to my clients, too, so that their journeys inspire them in life for wealth, health, and everything else in between. I recommend you make it a priority to read one of the books today!"
~ Goro Gupta, Chief Education Officer, Mortgage Terminator, Property Mentor.

"The *A Journey of Riches* book series is filled with real-life short stories of heartfelt tribulations turned into uplifting, self-transformation by the power of the human spirit to overcome adversity. The journeys captured in these books will encourage you to embrace life in a whole new way. I highly recommend reading this inspiring anthology series."
~ Chris Drabenstott, Best Selling Author and Editor.

"There is so much motivational power in the *A Journey of Riches* series!! Each book is a compilation of inspiring, real-life stories by several different authors, which makes the journey feel more relatable and success more attainable. If you are looking for something to move you forward, you'll find it in one (or all) of these books."
~ Cary MacArthur, Personal Empowerment Coach.

"I've been fortunate to write with John Spender, and now, I call him a friend. *A Journey of Riches* book series features real stories that have inspired me and will inspire you. John has a passion for finding amazing people from all over the world, giving the series a global perspective on relevant subject matters."
~ Mike Campbell, Fat Guy Diary, LLC.

"The *A Journey of Riches* series is the reflection of beautiful souls who have discovered the fire within. Each story takes you inside the truth of what truly matters in life. While reading these stories, my heart space expanded to understand that our most significant

contribution in this lifetime is to give and receive love. May you also feel inspired as you read this book."
~ Katie Neubaum, Author of *Transformation Calling*.

"*A Journey of Riches* is an inspiring testament that love and gratitude are the secret ingredients to living a happy and fulfilling life. This series is sure to inspire and bless your life in a big way. Truly an inspirational read that is written and created by real people, sharing real-life stories about the power and courage of the human spirit."
~ Jen Valadez, Emotional Intuitive and Best-Selling Author.

FOREWORD

By Kyle Zagrodzky

A group of highly successful people has gathered to refine and distill their wisdom and knowledge, built upon years of experience peppered with countless highs, lows, and self-doubt surrounding each of their journeys to bring you their secret to acquiring riches and mastering your mindset. The insights you can learn and integrate into your own life will no doubt serve you well because you have taken the time to read, reflect and incorporate the pearls of wisdom that await in the following pages. Pursuing a discipline of self-learning is a virtue and one I personally hold in high regard. I want to sincerely thank you for making an effort to be better tomorrow than you are today.

You already know that there are a lot of ways to make money. Some are faster, some are easier, some are rooted in one's passions, and others are sparked by a vision of creating something spectacular. Some become beautifully rich and successful across many areas of their lives, seemingly having little discernable capability or education to justify their achievements. In contrast, others are knowledgeable and possess the mental horsepower to rival all others. In truth, riches lie in wait for anyone and everyone. Whether you have skills, education, intelligence, resources, or none of the above, fortune favors the bold, the persistent, and the patient above all bright and shiny measures that society would have us believe.

Self-reliance and an unshakable mindset that you are worthy of whatever lofty goal you want to achieve are critical keys to success. It's the spark that builds to a slow burn, culminating over time into a raging fire of self-confidence. Your self-confidence, or unshakable certainty in the core of your being, serves you, the adventurer, who seeks to acquire riches in ways that are difficult to express. A deep-seated knowledge that your vision is worthy and that you are the one who will bring it forth is your shield against nay-sayers (and there will be many), over-whelming odds, or times of resource scarcity. Certainty in who you are is the foundation from which you will launch yourself towards your goal and guide you through the rough seas you will encounter on your journey.

Beyond the financial riches you may seek something even more valuable that I hope you savor along the way: wisdom. It's a peculiar thing that is only acquired through experience. The adventurer steps through fear and uncertainty and boldly charters the waters of the unknown.

Every decision you make with imperfect knowledge, every challenge you overcome, and every adversary you face offers nuggets of that invisible gift called wisdom. Each revelation you have turns you into a better, more capable version of yourself. Each of these is a tool that sharpens you and allows you to move faster as you learn to slice more effortlessly through every challenge you may encounter. You've most certainly experienced this feeling in many ways already. Circumstances that used to be overwhelming to you are hardly given a second thought now. Recognize it while it's happening and feel gratitude as you achieve this priceless gift.

The mindset is the driving force that holds future successes in focus above all else. Achievement is a game that is won and lost first and foremost in the mind. Emotions are real, regardless of whether others understand or feel the same way. Recognizing disempowering emotions or beliefs that may be swirling in your mind is hard for many, especially when you are feeling and focusing on them. Doing something about them during the low-energy or negative states they cause is even more challenging.

Mastering your emotions is an invaluable skill that will serve you above all others. Maintaining excitement and anticipation is the ultimate power. The writers that follow are masters in many ways. They will share techniques and strategies to disrupt negative emotions and replace them with high-energy excitement to drive you forward.

Congratulations to you, the adventurer, seeking more and taking action to achieve it. Your prize will be looking back on life in your old age with the pride that you took chances and made the most of the time you've been given.

TABLE OF CONTENTS

PREFACE

I collated this book and chose authors from around the world to share their experiences about what "*Master Your Mindset*" meant to them. The eclectic collection of chapters encompasses a myriad of different writing styles and perspectives that embrace the intelligence of our hearts and intuition.

Like all of us, each author has a unique story and insight to share with you. It might so happen that one or more authors have lived through an experience like one in your life. Their words could be just the words you need to read to help you through your challenges and motivate you to continue your chosen path.

Storytelling has been the way humankind has communicated ideas and learning throughout our civilization. While we have become more sophisticated with technology and life in the modern world is now more convenient, there is still much discontent and dissatisfaction. Many people have also moved away from reading books, and they are missing valuable information that can help them move forward in life with a positive outlook. Moving toward the tasks or dreams that scare us breeds confidence in growing towards becoming better versions of ourselves.

I think it is essential to turn off the television, slow down, read, reflect, and take the time to appreciate everything you have in life. Start with an anthology book as they offer a cornucopia of viewpoints relating to a particular theme. Here, it's fear and how others have dealt with it. I think we feel stuck in life or have challenges in a particular area because we see the problem through the same lens that created it. With this compendium and all the books in the *A Journey of Riches* series, you have many writing styles and perspectives that will help you think and see your challenges differently, motivating you to elevate your set of circumstances.

Anthology books are also great because you can start from any chapter and gain valuable insight or a nugget of wisdom without the feeling that you have missed something from the earlier episodes.

I love reading many types of personal development books because learning and personal growth are vital. If you are not learning and growing, well, you're staying the same. Everything in the universe is growing, expanding, and changing. If we are not open to different ideas and a multitude of ways to think and be, then even the most skilled and educated among us can become close-minded.

The concept of this book series is to open you up to diverse ways of perceiving your reality. It is to encourage and give you many avenues of thinking about the same subject. My wish for you is to feel empowered to make a decision that will best suit you in moving forward with your life. As Albert Einstein said, **"We cannot solve problems with the same level of thinking that created them."** With Einstein's words in mind, let your mood pick a chapter, or read from the beginning to the end and be guided to find the answers you seek.

If you feel inspired, we would love an honest review on Amazon. This will help create awareness around this fantastic series of books.

With gratitude,
John Spender

"Be the master of your mind and mentor of your thoughts."

~ Arya Senan

CHAPTER ONE

For What We Thin-kith We Become!

By Bec Bucci

Let's start with FEAR!

Before we can truly become the master of our mind, captain of our vessel, and the watchmaker of our soul gifted with an infinite, limitless ability to time travel through the metaverse, we must first recognize one very human characteristic that limits the potential of so many: Fear. There it is, that big ugly word. The habit of avoidance and feeling uncomfortable, the fear of letting go or leaning in. Whatever it means to you, it's the feeling that tells you to avoid, avoid, avoid at all costs. I know some of you felt uncomfortable just reading that word. I get it. I remember when I did too.

I was so awkward growing up, so much of a tomboy, that I was convinced I had been born the wrong sex altogether. I refused to wear dresses or play with Barbies and rode my BMX topless with all the boys until my breast buds started to pop out and I was forced to wear a t-shirt. I was so free back then, and yet, in adult-ing terms, quite exposed. I simply didn't give a hoot. Why? I hadn't been exposed to judgment, criticism, or ridicule, so I had nothing to fear when riding flat out down the hill, topless, hands off the handlebars and laughing with joy. My mindset was not polluted with social conditioning.

Over time, it can become part of our conditioning to stop standing out or speaking about this or that, and for goodness' sake, don't embarrass yourself. "Be a good girl/boy." So, it is no wonder I went on to become a Sexologist and Clinical Sexuality Coach. The more fun term is SEXPERT. I'm one little lady on a mission to absolutely shine the spotlight on the importance of self-expression, especially one's own sexual and sensual desires. After all, love is the drug that is more addictive than any other substance on the planet, reinforcing that at our core the human need for connection is a powerful force that, when channeled in its highest form, is more transcendental than any other synthetic substitute. Fully body orgasms all around, I say! That just shifted your mindset, didn't it?

We have far more power over how we experience the journey of being a human being than we are led to believe. So, while I do not have the personality type to blow my own trumpet, so to speak, it seems imperative to include in part and also to share what I've learned from my 25 years of professional experience working in the wellness space. Opening my first wellness and healing center at just 24 years old on the east coast of Australia was an ambitious and bold move, employing six staff (three psychologists, one physiotherapist, one Chinese medicine herbalist, and one massage therapist). On top, I cared for my partner and father to my daughter. He, at the time, had chronic fatigue syndrome, and I had to take over managing our fully functional permaculture farm while raising a newborn.

Most people thought I was mad, especially when I opened a second center 12 months later. The centers had a unique approach to creating a calm environment, and our treatment rooms ran off the main gallery that showcased photographic images of faces from around the globe. The theme of each exhibit was straightforward and always the same: Joy. Every photograph was designed to immediately evoke an emotional response at first glance as a reminder of love and genuine happiness. The gallery was also a drop-in space that included a free meditation room with a waterfall and stream running through the center. We called the center "Nature Within-Center for Stories" and it became a place to share and be seen. This is where my journey towards a better mindset began and where my first experience in witnessing how quickly the universe responds when the mind is clear, and the heart is calm. When we become truly aligned with our authentic selves and step forward with integrity resolutely, miracles become a reality, the impossible becomes possible, and the insurmountable becomes surmountable.

My first lesson in mastering the mind led me to challenge my beliefs around this concept. I continually tell myself this: If I can imagine anything in its perfect state, there is no barrier to its creation. In that very moment in time, it already exists. All I have to do in the first instance is believe. If you want to harness your natural flow in attracting the universe's abundance, which is just waiting for your invitation in order to gift you everything you need, you must first believe that it is possible. If I had listened those many years ago to all the reasons why my very first center would fail, I never would have opened the doors to what has been an incredible adventure, and one that has ultimately shaped me into the woman I am today.

However, belief requires a little assistance from several other mindset components to create the perfect recipe to successfully manifest that which delivers the highest net worth value into your human experience. First believe that you are capable. As much as I have been the facilitator, the mentor, the coach, the therapist, the healer, and the seer, I have also been, throughout each experience, the consummate observer, the witness, the scribe, and forever the humble understudy—perspective and perception dance side by side in the quest to master the mind. Becoming capable is reflected by our choices, these lead us to experience higher levels of consciousness or to lead us away. So to raise the frequency of our vibrational pull and, in turn, our ability to attract what we truly need and desire into our orbital self-universe, we must ACT.

BELIEVE that you are capable and ACT on that WISDOM.

When we act, we are moving through the distraction that can hold us back from truly experiencing all the juiciness that life has to offer. It is only when we embrace fear as a precursor to the start of an extraordinary breakthrough that we can become practiced in mastering our emotional responses from a balanced state of being. The faster we act, the easier it becomes for the universe to deliver what we need.

The art of detachment is a mastery within itself; however, this skill is the key to managing and mastering your fear and, ultimately, your mindset. So, let's talk about becoming fearless over becoming fear stuck. Will we ever become completely fearless? Well, the answer really depends on you. We should, of course, have a healthy respect for those situations that could cause us harm, which relates to having a sense of wisdom about what is beneficial for us, but that is a little different from a fearless mind. Practicing detachment is an exercise in self-control.

It's easy for the ego self to find meaning in just about anything that will reinforce our belief system; both in ways that serve us and in ways that do not. This leads us to the requirement of being honest about our soul goals and define what is healthy for us. Reinforcing states that maintain a peaceful mind, the people we surround ourselves with, the environments we allow ourselves to be exposed to, and the level of conversations we have with others all influence our state of being. Making sure all of the above is healthy becomes a matter of responsibility and of being reasonable with oneself.

We are making choices continuously and our synapses are firing at lightning speeds, moving faster across the neurological pathways than superman could ever fly around the planet whilst rewinding the fabric of time. So, taking reasonable steps to slow down long enough to quieten the chatter means taking responsibility for one's well-being. If we are to speak about fear and the ability to let go of what holds us back, we must also talk about love.

Are you ready to love?

Having mastery over the mind requires daily rituals that let us hit "reset". A positive mindset needs your perspective to be valued and valuable. Unity, free from separation, allows for self-acceptance of the current state you are experiencing. Your ability to remain in that state or let it go depends on how well you allow and accept love, of self and others. We can shift gears very quickly when we respond to our lower nature with love in mind. We can distinguish this more clearly in others. When we acknowledge these imperfections within ourselves, our empathy grows exponentially, and we realize that we no longer need to take things personally. You must be ready to love it all, for when we shift to this mindset, we begin to understand and experience detachment on a whole new level. This creates freedom for the self and space for others to be in unity with the present moment.

Are you ready for love?

Fear and love are the two motivating forces that can make us feel uncomfortable. The Yin and Yang, the dark and the light have a purpose in journeying to our deepest calling. If the call is based on integral truth, every calling has a sense. If we want to change the world, we must focus on our inner church. I want you to sit with this concept: Imagine your soul is a temple. Take a moment, close your eyes, and visualize what your perfect and peaceful place of contentment looks like. Allow yourself to feel your ideal world and build that in your mind. Perhaps it's on the edge of cliffs with waves crashing, on the top of a mountain, in the amazon rain forest, or deep within an underground cave. Does your temple have walls, windows, or maybe none at all? Are there people in your temple, or is it still? I call this place of wisdom the seat of the soul.

For many of us, before we wake up to what I like to call the Great Mystery and start to experience an enlightened version of ourselves, we must journey back to the place of self-love. We must accept that we are not for everyone and that everyone is not for us. That takes a dose of courage to detach from opinions, forcing us to recognize what is not meant for us and identifying what we need to flow towards that will elevate us. Be mindful of those who sit at the bottom of the mountain with you but do not wish to make the climb to the top in order to celebrate alongside you. Let go and Let Love In.

Mastering the mind is as much about accepting the existence of peace as it is about letting go. We can let go, with love, in the wisdom that we exist in the universe as a myriad of atoms occupying this space as matter. In our case, as the soul inhabits the avatar, the avatar is transitory, the soul eternal, so nothing is ever truly lost, nor is it ever irretrievable. However, nothing is as it appears, so let go and allow the mystery in. Self-love welcomes the passage of forgiveness, which becomes your key to the door that will open and allow your mind to elevate to a state of presentness.

Once we establish the balance between love and fear, we can discern between that which is accurate and that which is not — remembering that the ego self can be persuasive when it comes to avoiding something that may appear potentially painful at some point in the future or remind us of an experience that created those same feelings of discomfort. This is where the power to reset the mind becomes a vital tool in moving into a state of staying present. But how do we remain present?

By knowing what we need and by asking for what we want. This is an inside job, by the way.

Ask yourself two questions…

Do I know what I need?

Do I know what I want to achieve?

You see, the mind is happiest when it has a detailed description and a clear direction to where and what it should focus on. Without that, the mind will focus on just about anything as a simple act of looking for reasoning and a way to apply meaning. Meaning creates a sense of perceived and justifiable safety. That is why some needs and wants show up in our lives in ways that are almost everything we are looking for, but don't quite fully hit the mark.

If you are unsure of what you truly need and want to achieve, my loving solution is to start from the very beginning. Reflection done in a calm and meditative state opens the doorway for divine wisdom to enter the heart and the mind. We create unity and balance when we connect the heart and the mind. When we build harmony and balance, we can consciously induce a state of love and joy. As we start to ascend into a place of unconditional love for the self, and this state of "be-ing" begins to be experienced as pure inner joy. It is no longer simply a pleasurable response to an experience or event that is dependent on external factors taking place. Our alternative perception is to experience joy as a constant companion to every moment as it occurs. Once elevated within this realm, we have an immense capacity to extend patience even in the face of adversity, whether brief or prolonged, we can maintain a positive attitude.

This is where our individual "will" combines with divine "will". The start of a journey of compassion that allows the soul to see that everything in this world is, in fact, an expression of Love and Divinity. To become clear on how to follow the path of divine existence, we must become open to receiving. All feedback is critical in edging us closer to owning our inner truth: that we are a miraculous phenomenon simply because we are a presence. When this truth permeates and pierces through the individual state of being, we experience effortless synchronicities that alter one's sense of responsibility away from the individual and towards the celebration of life itself. This is where the magic starts to happen and leads to my final agreement shared at the end of this chapter.

So far, we have established four agreements that we need to make with ourselves to master our mindset. First, we will need to be committed to leaning into the following:

Agreement One

Fearlessness.

Agreement Two

Self-love and the act of detachment.

Agreement Three

Knowing what I need.

Agreement Four

Knowing what I want to achieve.

These agreements, of course, are endless and renew themselves time and time again as we grow and ascend into higher states of consciousness. We cannot know what we do not know until we know what we did not.

How do we know it?

Agreement Five - be ready and commit to not compromising your standards. Stop making excuses for yourself and others. Do not lower your expectations to fit in with the world. The soul is not a slave to the mind; albeit we are led to believe that this is true, it is indeed the opposite. The soul is your driver, and the mind operates the vehicle that leads you to your desired destination. Just like driving a car, it does not force you to take to the wheel. You drive it. When you get in, you know where you are going and which route to take to get there. Approach setting your mindset in the same fashion, and you will forever be in control of the outcome. Setting your standards is like entering the details into your internal GPS to keep you on track. When your criteria become clear, you will not notice the distractions or lend yourself to being distracted.

Agreement Six - Set clear boundaries. Have the conversation up front with yourself first. Be clear on your expectations because these ultimately will define your outcomes. Define the terms of the agreement that you are holding yourself to and commit to holding yourself accountable to those terms within a specific time frame. The truth is, you will mess up along the way; however, you can quickly reset your mindset by deploying the instrument of catch and release. Just because it is thrown your way doesn't mean you must catch and hold onto it. If it sits outside your boundaries, simply release it.

Over many years of journeying, I have developed a very simple acronym. It reminds me to free myself from the BARS of the mind. To seek solutions that lead to resolutions that expand my human experience and deliver me into a state ever closer to the divine form of eternal contentment.

Believe it is possible

Act on it

Receive with gratitude

Surrender your will

BARS are not real; they are self-imposed by the individual operating and relating to the world as an "individual" that exists in a separate reality from the human experience. Yet, once we release our grip on these BARS, a harmonious unfoldment, detached from outcomes, will manifest truly wondrous potentialities free from power and ones forged in love, ultimately orchestrating the ascension symphony that will elevate the mind into the mindset state of unlimited freedom. Freedom permits us to relinquish our limiting beliefs; by forfeiting our attachment to these limiting beliefs, we can let go of any residual shame, doubts, fears, insecurities, disappointments, failures and so on. This allows for endless possibilities and progressively higher opportunities to resonate in a constant state of joy and ecstasy.

Agreement Seven - Surrender. Divine providence, omniscient, omnipotent, or all-powerful, the divine source knows all truths and all falsehoods. A fully mastered mindset can lead you to transcend it together, where the soul is no longer dictated by the identity of the personality you may believe you are. That is why we refer to Buddha as a Master, for example, the ability to transcend the human personality into ethereal wisdom. I believe anything is possible when we lower our heads and bow down in peaceful providence.

Surrendering is not a one-step process and has many intricate facets to its authentic reunification. I could write a whole book on the Power of Surrendering, but for now, I will share the starting steps that came to me all those years ago when I opened my first wellness center.

It was a time of great surrender for me back then, a complete de-robbing that left me standing naked, fully exposed to the elements of my life that appeared to be occurring entirely outside of my control. It was only when I understood the basic principles of surrendering your "will" completely to divine providence that I came to understand the impact of the presumptive principles of dualistic causation and affect that so many of us apply when being attached to what is good and what is bad, more so our precursor to respond identically or similarly. In basic terms regarding the laws of the universe, nothing is ever really happening to us but for us.

This self-realization becomes progressively present when our "knowingness" becomes recognized as Divinity and the world is no longer seen simply as it appears but rather for its radiance of the essence that is endlessly provided to us by the source. Here's the real jaw clencher: the outcome matters not.

Any significant transformation requires adherence to the modalities of faith, devotion and surrender.

Faith - believe in.

Devotion - act on.

Surrender - your will.

Start small with small acts of letting go. Hand it over to the source. Here you go, please take this and so be it. The more we practice this act of letting small things go, the greater capacity we will have to master the mind and the sharing in of the moment we are experiencing right now. As you read these words on the page, you are with me, and I am with you. Our pure existence eternally connects us.

In closing, remember that fear is not accurate. You can let go of the BARS, you have the power to quieten the mind and you can surrender your "will" if you so choose.

Remember:

Practice makes perfect.

Be a work in constant progress.

Be brave and dare to surrender your will.

You will need courage. You are attempting to do what many will not, and that is to follow your soul's calling and live your life to its fullest potential. You will need to make the necessary adjustments, and this requires commitment. This will also require bravery because the very nature of living your greatest adventure leading to a life of freedom requires you take a daily practice. This creates more choices that require a higher level of discernment regarding what you need and what you wish to achieve on the path to mastery.

Shine.

Lastly, please remember to shine bright. This doesn't mean cast a shadow on others. Instead, invite them to share the afterglow. The sun and moon have a mutual respect for each other, and so they effortlessly move out of the way for the other. They are not in competition. Instead, it is a delicate balance between night and day and day and night. They allow space for the other to cast their light in support of rest and growth; they are not attached to outcomes, even if the stars cannot be seen without them.

What we think,

We become.

What we believe,

We attract.

When we act on,

We achieve.

When we Surrender

We are FREE to "🐝»

"When you go from a fixed mindset to a growth mindset, a new world of possibilities opens up."

~ Imaan Farooq

CHAPTER TWO

Activating Level 10 GRIT

By Kyle Zagrodzky

Author, Husband, Father, Leader

GRIT: A personality trait possessed by individuals who demonstrate passion and perseverance toward a goal despite being confronted by significant obstacles and distractions. Those with grit can self-regulate and postpone their need for positive reinforcement while working diligently on a task.

Books, TED Talks, and business coaches speak of grit as the secret to success. Many have concluded that grit is a far better predictor of success than all other measures. However, what I am about to share with you is unique and likely something you have never even heard of before. I am about to share with you the very source of grit and how to activate it with yourself!

Where does it come from? If you have it, why? If you don't, how do you get it?

In short, without it, success is still possible but quite difficult when the headwinds ensue, especially for entrepreneurs.

Who am I to even be covering this topic? Well, by almost all societal measures, I shouldn't be successful. So please allow me to introduce myself. I share the following not to impress you nor feed any need for my significance. I am simply sharing the following so you will understand the utter contrast between who I am versus what I have achieved.

As I am writing this, I am 53-years-old. I have a wife of 27 years whom I love more than the day I said, "I do." She is my best friend and someone I can talk to about anything. In addition, we have three teenage sons. They get along amazingly well, and they, too, can talk about anything with us without fear of judgment. Since my late teenage years, I've boot-strapped many businesses, which is to say I have self-funded them to a large extent. My companies have earned well over 100 million U.S. dollars, span the globe, and I have employed thousands of people. I've traveled to more than 30 countries. World-famous Tony Robbins, the most successful life and business coach in history, became a friend and business partner in my company, OsteoStrong, in 2017.

I have spoken to audiences of between 10,000 and 20,000 people worldwide. I have developed close relationships with powerful, well-known people around the world. My life has been quite a journey, in fact, a rare journey indeed. So, I've been successful in my marriage, with the raising of my sons, and in my businesses. Many people have achieved these things and written books about what they've learned along the way. So, what's the difference? Let's look at what I had to work with when I started my journey of riches. First, I'm dyslexic, which makes reading hard for me. It's very frustrating and requires a lot of focus to get my mind to properly follow the normal left-to-right reading pattern, one line at a time. Fortunately, I love reading and have learned a lot from books. But, to this day, I struggle with even reading a teleprompter, the screen that feeds the speaker small, bite-sized chunks of words at a time.

Eventually, I just ditched the teleprompters and now I memorize everything for any speaking event or recording that requires exact wording. Reading legal contracts and complicated documents that require focus and precision takes an extraordinary effort, and I employ unique techniques that many others with dyslexia use. These techniques have greatly improved my ability to focus and after a lot of practice, I am able to read a little faster.

To make matters even more challenging, I also have attention deficit disorder (ADD) and have struggled with focusing on even the simplest things, for most of my life. My mind always feels like it's in overdrive with a never-ending, multi-threaded past, present, and future analysis. But having ADD and dyslexia were not my only challenges. When I was 14-years-old, my father went bankrupt. Back then and through college, I was a C student, and since my parents had no money as well as challenges of their own, I worked two to three jobs at a time to pay for my education and all of my expenses.

And there were yet more challenges: As a young man, I lived with many deep-seated visceral fears. I was terrified of heights, public speaking, flying on a plane, talking to girls I found attractive, and I had an unhealthy fear of failure and of being judged by others. In college, I was terrified of the future and had no idea what I wanted to do after graduation or if anyone would hire me. I was probably one of the last people you would have guessed would make anything of themselves. I was, however, fantastic at covering up my many shortcomings from everyone. Not even my parents knew I had any of these struggles. I can confidently state that I did not find success from my education, financial resources, or innate skills. Looking back, I can see clearly that my current reality and all that I have achieved was the orphaned offspring of grit.

So, when I pondered the concept of grit, I thought long and hard about what value I could offer you in a single chapter that may have a meaningful impact on your journey of riches. I surmised that no one wants to hear about what grit is, instead, I suspected readers would like to know how to acquire it. So, I considered people in my past who were more intelligent than me, had more money, more charisma, massive confidence, and a stellar education who had achieved far less. The first thing I considered was that maybe they feared failure too much to take risks or were perhaps too concerned about the judgment of others. Maybe it was a lack of resources, or they calculated that the risk versus reward was too significant. Those are sound reasons, but that couldn't be it. I had those fears and challenges as well. So, what was it? What was the source of my perseverance, my willingness to make frequent out-of-the-box decisions followed by massive action, often without enough resources and usually without the skills or experience needed to know how I would fully execute?

But as I was in deep contemplation, searching my heart and reviewing the experiences of my life, I discovered the Holy Grail: the source of grit. I believe it's available to anyone who wants it. And with it comes an amazing life well-spent and, of course, riches.

So, allow me to set up an analogy for you that will help me to prove my point. Earlier this year I turned on Netflix and stumbled across a reality series called *Alone*. It seemed like an intriguing concept, and there was a total of 8 seasons, so I figured it had stood the test of time and would probably be a good way to enjoy a relaxing Saturday evening with my wife. The concept of the show was that the producers would recruit ten experienced survivalists and take each of them to a secluded location in the wilderness. Each survivalist was left entirely alone, allowing them to have only ten simple survival items. The winner of the experience is the one who survives in the wilderness the longest. That rugged soul wins $500,000 USD. These challenges can go on for about two to four months until only one person remains. In season 8, the one we started with, these ten amazing people were taken to a remote part of western Canada known to have a high grizzly bear population. As time passed, people started dropping out for various reasons. As the contestants dwindled, and more than a month had passed, one of the contestants commented that one of the things that made continuing with the challenge so difficult was a device they were given when they were dropped off.

It was a hand-held communicator with a button they could press at any time. Upon activating it, the production team would race rescuers out to extract the bewildered survivalist, bringing them back to the safety and comfort of base camp. In times of distress, despair, or failure, the ever-present "tap-out" button was always within reach of each contestant. Access to this option made grinding through the challenges and loneliness even harder. For the adventurer seeking riches, one of the first keys to attaining grit is to understand what your personal hard-wired tap-out technique is and then destroy it utterly. There can be no way out. Once you cut off all possibilities of escape, you become resourceful in ways you can't imagine. It is most certainly a "burn-the-boats" mindset. If you're going to invade a stronghold on land from the sea and you burn your boats before the battle, victory or death are the only two remaining options.

Earlier, I stated that fear of failure and judgment are two things most people live with. Knowing how you have protected yourself from self-judgment or the judgment of others in any past life or business failure is essential to understand. This is likely your favored tap-out strategy. Because if the cause of failure can be deflected onto something or someone else, surrender won't lead to emotional pain or regret. Most will choose this prevalent "tap-out" strategy as their go-to when failure seems imminent. I call this the EXCUSES or BLAMING "tap-out" method. It's also sometimes referred to as the fundamental attribution error.

Someone looking to tap-out wants to protect themselves from judgment and they will come up with excuses that they believe make it impossible to achieve their goal. They will then share these reasons with others to protect themselves as a means of deflecting judgment. In business, it usually goes like this: I ran out of money, the economy entered a recession, a significant competitor moved in, I had lazy employees, I was hit with a frivolous lawsuit, etc. Those all seem like reasonable and very believable excuses. But as an adventurer seeking riches or an extraordinary life, you must confront the reality that these excuses simply aren't good enough. For the one who has burnt the boats, adversity will spawn resourcefulness and a way forward is almost always found. History is filled with success stories against all odds. I know because I'm one of them, and if you can think of any business-killing challenge, I'm pretty sure I've come up against it many times.

The cure for this tap-out technique is adopting a mindset of extreme ownership. A book on extreme ownership that I highly recommend *is Extreme Ownership: How U.S. Navy SEALs Lead and Win* by Jocko Willink and Leif Babin. It does a great job of explaining the depths of this concept. In SEALs training (also called BUD/S), they are taught that no matter what unfortunate situation they may find themselves in, their response must always be an enthusiastic, "good!" In essence, everything that causes you pain in any area of your life is to be faced with a grateful attitude. No matter what gets thrown at you, it's now your responsibility, rather, your *opportunity* to find the hidden solution and to ferociously take massive action, without complaint. We experience the most growth when we live through challenges instead of avoiding them. So, step one to achieving grit is to identify what your default tap-out technique is and prepare yourself to take extreme ownership of all obstacles that you may encounter.

The "why" behind my grit comes from a fear of judgment and failure. I come from a family of brilliant people. My father earned a degree in chemical engineering from MIT, the most prestigious engineering school in the United States, if not the world, then he went to Stanford to earn an MBA, all while working multiple jobs to pay his way because he came from a poor farming family. He and my mom had four sons. I am the youngest. My oldest brother speaks fluent French and Spanish, earned an MBA from the Wharton School of Business, and was elected president of the student body. My second oldest brother was first in his class at Harvard Medical School and became an electrophysiologist, a highly technical cardiology specialty. And my third oldest brother became a fantastic lawyer from a prestigious Texas university while earning the privilege of serving on the school's law review.

Finally, there's me. You know most of my foundational challenges already.

Throughout all my years in school, from elementary to college, my family thought I was lazy. As a result, the story I told myself was that to be loved, I needed to work extremely hard and achieve academic excellence. I believed that failing at anything I did would only be a confirmation of the "lazy" label. To fail meant I would be the disappointment that I was expected to be. Since I couldn't earn good grades in school, my only other option was always working hard to be worthy of love. I would rather die trying to achieve my goals than fail at them. Seriously. Death would have been more accessible than the emotional pain of failure. That may sound extreme, however, humans always do more to avoid pain than to achieve pleasure. Success isn't about having more riches to me. Though it's a nice little byproduct of what I do, it has always been about being worthy of love. If people are honest, the pain of not being loved is unbearable. For a man, love means a few things, but being respected is number one.

So, after reading my story, did you see the final key to a grit mindset? It is this:

GRIT comes from pain.

"Burning the boats" is much more than a fun quip thrown around in motivational speeches. It must become your reality. With it, you will have the knowledge that you will *always* find the solution to whatever challenge is laid at your feet.

The Adventurer's Creed:

There is ALWAYS a solution to EVERYTHING.

I love the story of Captain John Paul Jones. He was a Scottish-born American captain of the U.S. warship *Bon Homme Richard* (named after Benjamin Franklin) during the American Revolutionary War against the British. While at sea, he came head-to-head with the more powerful English warship HMS *Serapis* off the North Sea. During the three-hour battle, his ship was being pummeled by gunfire. The British officer asked Captain Jones if he was ready to surrender. A tap-out option seemed like the only choice given the circumstances. He was sinking and defeat was imminent. But for Captain Jones, failure was worse than death. The tap-out option wasn't one he could accept. Ultimately, his superpower of extreme ownership was activated, and the solution to this unwinnable situation presented itself. He shouted to the British commander the famous and often quoted phrase: "I have not yet begun to fight!" He steered his vessel and smashed it into the British ship, ordering his men to board and engage the British sailors in hand-to-hand combat. The British crew surrendered, the Americans won the battle, raised the American flag on the British ship, and sailed the British ship back to America! It's an amazing story by all accounts and one that often inspires me in the face of any adversary. It's a beautiful portrait of situational grit.

I will give my friend and mentor, Tony Robbins, some serious props here. While I had plenty of grit before it became a subject matter in today's modern business and personal development landscape, I never knew from where it came or that I even had grit. I thought it was simply who I was and who I am now. Those with hardcore grit have a powerful emotional trigger deep in the foundation of their soul that, when activated, not even the gates of hell will stand against them. When I attended my first Tony Robbins event back in 2016, I was in absolute awe as I watched a true master in every sense of the word, lead thousands of people through a process designed to create the very emotional foundation that inspires grit to help drive people to achieve a specific goal or overcome a challenge. I had never seen or experienced anything like this in my life. He called it the Dicken's Process. It's a process inspired by Charles Dickens' *A Christmas Carol*. In the story, Scrooge, is an unhappy, uncaring individual that generally treats everyone in his life poorly. He goes to bed one Christmas Eve and encounters three different ghosts in a dream: The Ghost of Christmas Past, The Ghost of Christmas Present, and the Ghost of Christmas Future. Each ghost shows him a different perspective of certain events in his life that slowly begins to help him realize that his actions have had painful outcomes. The final ghost, the Ghost of Christmas Future, was the tipping point and the key to his ultimate transformation. This ghost showed him a future that he was manifesting through his present actions that would eventually lead to more pain, misery, and his eventual death. His future self and current attitude became disgusting, and when he awoke, he was a changed man, loving, caring and generous. Tony has led millions of people through this process designed to attach negative emotions to failing to succeed. This event is called Unleash the Power Within.

Are you lacking grit? Do you want it? Do you see a future version of yourself mercilessly kicking down barriers in your path toward victory without fear or hesitation? I'll admit, I can't imagine a life without the ever-present feeling of infinite solutions to all problems and certain success in everything I set my mind to. However, I think it's fitting at this point that I share a word of caution with you. You need to be prepared for potential costs once you unleash your level 10 inner lion. There are some strategies you may want to consider as you unlock your unstoppable grit power.

As previously mentioned, I am the father of three sons. Most parents can agree that if their children's lives were ever in danger, nothing would stop them from doing everything in their power to save them. The world recently saw an example of a mother in Uvalde, Texas, who pushed past the police to rush into a school with an active shooter to save her children. So, I want you to first imagine for a moment that the lives of your children (or any other significant person in your life) depended on you succeeding at your goal or overcoming your challenge. When in that state, nothing else matters, right? *Nothing*. Your goal must be achieved because the outcome of failure would be unbearable. When you successfully destroy your "tap-out" mechanisms and anchor future pain of failure to your goal, you may become so fixated on achieving your outcome that other aspects of your life suffer. Grit is a lion and unbridled can turn on you in ways you may not be prepared for. So, I felt it necessary, as I share the secrets to activating grit, that I also equip you with some strategies and tools to both protect you and accelerate you along your journey.

I share the following, not to influence your beliefs but to illustrate that having complete certainty of the following topic generates a massive amount of peace through the storms of business and life. First, I need to tell you a little bit more about me, and I share the following only because without it, I could not have achieved what I have. I was raised as an agnostic, which is to say that I had no beliefs about God one way or the other. After graduating high school, I knew almost nothing about religions. At some point in my 20s, I began seeking a deeper meaning to this weird and unexplainable life. As I started my journey, I didn't know what I would find, and I was a little fearful. There was so much to learn, and everything surrounding the topic of God had so many varying and conflicting opinions from very well-read, educated people. As I began seeking answers to just about every hard question I could think of, I refused to set my beliefs on anything I couldn't conclude as absolute truth. I have learned and have seen many times that whatever a person declares as truth invariably becomes their identity. Humans will staunchly defend our identity, sometimes even to our death. After about ten years of intensive questioning and research, the data I had gathered and the amazing things I had experienced painted me into a truth corner, and I became a follower of Jesus Christ.

Because of that journey, I now have an unwavering belief in a Creator. Knowing this has served me and brought clarity to every other piece of secular wisdom I have gained. I believe that God knew my name when he spoke the universe into existence and this still leaves me in awe. In the mightiest of storms, I feel complete and at peace. I am very much aware that you may not believe what I believe, nor did I for half of my life. If you do not, I make no judgments about you, nor do anyone's beliefs about a creator influence how I feel about them. You don't need faith in a creator or Jesus to find grit.

The second word of caution: grit can create a sense of over-confidence or impatience, especially when your future outcome becomes a crystal-clear reality in your mind fueled by do-or-die emotion. The following is a series of questions I frequently ask myself, as well as tactics and perspectives that help remind me that I may have gaps in my capability and understanding. They also help me stay grounded and to appreciate my capabilities, the work of others, and the relationships I have made. These are your antidotes to the previously mentioned challenges you may face:

GUIDING QUESTIONS

1. What am I not seeing?
2. Who can help me and how can I add value to them?
3. How can I leave this situation or this individual better than I found them?
4. What meaning am I assigning to this situation? What could it mean?

"Nothing has any meaning, but we ASSIGN meaning to everything."
– Tony Robbins

THINK BEFORE YOU GRIT

Before going through the exercise of lighting the emotional fires of level 10 grit, you need absolute clarity on what you want. I suggest asking yourself these questions:

1. If resources were not an issue and I had the people, finances, and everything else I needed to execute my dream fully, how far would I take this dream? What would be my ultimate utopian outcome?

   It's important not to think of the "how" when visualizing the answer to this question, but rather focus only on the best-desired outcome.

2. Once you have the perfect outcome in mind, imagine all the good things that will happen because you achieve your goals. Write them down and feel the emotional satisfaction of what achievement means. Savor those emotions and meditate on them. Feel appreciation and gratitude for all you accomplish and how many lives will be impacted.

3. Imagine the worst possible future if you never try or eventually give up on your dream. See yourself years into the future and imagine the highest level of pain you can cause yourself and others should you fail. See every relationship that will be destroyed, people that will be let down, and the disappointment you will feel in yourself. Feel all those future feelings of having failed deeply. Create the level ten pain that would fuel a parent willing to face a deranged gun-wielding madman to save their child. Once you have successfully created that emotional pain and burned those images in your mind, it becomes your grit trigger. God help anyone or anything that stands in your way!

The Prospect of Future Emotional Pain Should You Fail is the source of your GRIT.

The Joy of Victory is One of the Countless Rewards that Await You!

Grit is genuine, and with it, people have accomplished extraordinary things. My sincere desire is that I have served you well. I appreciate you on so many levels for taking the time to expand your perspective. Your life is a canvas, and you are the artist. Make something unique with the time you've been given, my friend. Riches await you!

"With the right mindset, we can't lose, we either practice what we've learned or we learn what we need to practice."

~ Noura

CHAPTER THREE

The Breakthrough With An Elevated Mindset

By Dr. Olga Zabora, PsyD

"I believe I can fly, I believe I can touch the sky.

I think about it night and day,

spread my wings and fly away…" (song by R. Kelly)

This dedication is to all my clients that I have had the opportunity to work with and was able to witness your growth, your tears, and your greatest successes. It is my honor to guide you through those sacred journeys so that you have chosen to have the courage to walk this path! Much love and many blessings to all of you.

Dr. Olga Zabora, PsyD

We've all heard that we cannot solve a problem with the same mind that created it, haven't we?

Then how do we solve it? First, we need to recognize the stuck state and then elevate our thinking with the right mindset, creating the conditions for the breakthrough and solidifying the changes to live powerfully in a resourceful state. As it was proven that the main ingredient for change is the right mindset.

My experience working with clients shows that three mindsets could take place in the process of transformation: Survival Mindset, Unlimited Mindset and Intentional Mindset. These are like rooms in your internal house that can be used at different times in your life. Though they are different facets of the same crystal.

The Survival Mindset can be kicked in during extreme life-and-death situations – like when my friend, Lea went swimming with a boogie board on a sunny day in Maui and almost drowned while being hit by a great wave. While she was swimming to the surface of the ocean, her mind started to spin in a different direction, towards the depths of negativity: "This is how people drown and die!" she thought. Yet she was able to shake off the fear by thinking: "Focus on what you want – you want to get to the shore no matter what. No matter if the wave is big or small, you are going to make it." It felt to her like an eternity. Time had disappeared, leaving just stillness inside and one single thought: "I'm going to make it." Her single thought focus and mindset helped her to survive the life-and-death edge.

The Unlimited Mindset is used when we use our creative abilities to manifest our goals. By daydreaming, or by being in a relaxed state or light trance, or being in hypnosis, we can create healing in our body or manifest the life we want – like manifesting a beach house by drawing it or creating a vision board, like so many people I witnessed.

The Intentional Mindset is utilized when you learn how to create the conditions for your mind to make positive changes. You can learn this on your own, or with a guide or coach who knows how the mind works and can teach the shortcuts for achieving the greatest success with the right mindset. In this process you create the goals, reframe negative thinking to a positive one, creating the resourceful states. The following story is a vivid example of one woman's breakthrough from having a disempowered and stuck state to the best version of herself using an Unlimited and Intentional mindset that allowed her to create the life she always wanted.

The following story will let you see that long-lasting, positive changes are possible when the right mindset and mind power are present. In order to get the success and results, the best format for the Mindset Breakthrough Coaching Sessions is when the sessions are done over a couple of months, with follow-up sessions spread out over a few more weeks. It helps to solidify the changes that occur during the intense coaching work, and then you learn how to "live" your Best Version of Yourself.

Disclaimer: These are the highlights of the Breakthrough Coaching Session Program, which is always tailored to individual clients. The description of the coaching client is modified to keep privacy and confidentiality.

PART ONE: HOW TO FILL YOUR BUCKET LIST BY RECOGNIZING A LIMITED MINDSET

Dealing with pain…

After tying one of her last stripes, and having the cameras on her gliding wings checked by the assistant, Carrie started to run off the cliff. Seeing the beautiful lush green mountains and blue water (her favorite colors), she took off and began to glide over Rio with freedom and tears of happiness streaming down her rosy cheeks. All she "saw" in her mind was the emerald ring shining far beyond the horizon, reminding her that a new goal and new state were achievable, along with new strength and courage as well: "I am flying over Rio!" screamed Carrie. She knew that she was living the Best Version of Herself…

Six months earlier:

Carrie dialed the phone number, hoping that nobody would pick up and she would not have to leave a message. But a friendly voice answered:

"Dr. Zabora, speaking, how may I help you to change your life for the better today?"

"*Today? Is it possible to change it all?*" The question went through Carrie's mind and she felt the heat coming up her face. With shaking hands she almost pressed the off button but something made her stay. Maybe it was the tiredness of her always being shy, and not acting on or stepping up when she wanted to say something or express her emotions of love and gratitude.

This time, she decided it was her chance to change things for good. So she answered: "My dog is dying…" and burst into tears.

"I'm sorry to hear that; you dialed the wrong number. I am a doctor, but I think you need to get to a vet clinic," I replied.

"I know, I need help…" said Carrie, swallowing her tears. "I need *your* help." She slowly composed herself and continued: "I'd like to know if I can change the way I do things. I want to participate in a marathon, and I want to change my life. I can't stay at my current job. I want to connect with friends without worrying about what they will say after I express my voice and opinions. And I'd like to fly over Rio!" She stopped right after this, as though it sounded so delusional. She did not believe her goals were possible at all, especially after blurting everything right at the get-go. Carrie anxiously waited to hear the comforting voice, and wished for hope…

"Yes. It is possible with courage and perseverance. Everything is possible with the right mindset," I replied. "Only if you are ready for the changes and take responsibility for your new life…"

"I can't continue to live in this pain anymore," Carrie said.

"When can you come over for the first meeting, set the goals for your transformational journey, and learn what it takes for you to get there?" I asked.

"Whenever the first day is available!" rapidly replied Carrie.

"I have just opened the window for Friday at two pm. And please let me know if you need a good vet to care for your dog."

"I have a good one," Carrie said. "I'm taking him to the veterinarian today. I'll be at your office on Friday at two pm. Thank you, doctor."

Carrie came to the office fifteen minutes earlier than scheduled, and waited anxiously for her Goal Setting Session. She wrote her goals down in case she'd forget them or be too anxious to say them. She looked to be in her early thirties, and was slim and tall, with beautiful greenish eyes matching her skin color, and golden-red curly hair tied on top of her head in a ponytail. Her puffy eyes were red from crying and her face was pale with freckles. She was dressed in a gray sweatshirt and sports pants that hung on her very loosely. She wore no jewelry, just a tiny emerald ring on her pinky finger. The only bright elements about her were her sneakers, a charming fit. When I mentioned them, she replied that wearing good and comfortable running shoes was important because she was a runner and swimmer. I noticed that she was nervously playing with a rubber band. I asked if she knew the rubber band could be used for her benefit.

Even though everything hinted that she had a stuck mindset, she was surprisingly receptive to hearing more about the technique, which was to put the rubber band on her wrist and snap it (not too hard) when she caught herself spiraling down into negative thinking. The goal was to "snap yourself out" of the negative trance. It became the first technique she discovered that day, that worked amazingly well.

As I learned later, Carrie had been born in Australia, and her parents had moved to the United States when she was around two years old. She was still living in her parents' house. She had two dogs: one was an eleven-and-a-half-year-old basset who had back joint issues, could not go for long walks, and needed extra care.

He was on a special diet and was not eating well, so the feeding process was like taking care of a baby. Sometimes, injections needed to be done. This was Carrie's favorite dog, as she had raised him since he was a puppy. They had so many fun times together, and her anxiety was through the roof, knowing he could die at any time. She wondered if she would be able to cope with the transition. Carrie had another dog: a chihuahua female rescue dog around three years old and happy like a puppy that Carrie had gotten last year. That chihuahua was giving her some comfort and "brightened her days."

Carrie and I talked in my office for about an hour. Then, with her guard finally down she breathed out loudly and forcefully, and said: "That's it."

I offered her chamomile tea and let her stay in that "empty," full potential state. When she was bringing her painful and stuck conditions to the "table," her speech had been significantly influenced by the limited thinking. But by speaking up in the right environment, Carrie made the space inside that she could now fill with the new way of thinking that could propel her forward in life. She could focus on what she wanted instead of what she carried inside herself before.

When I asked her if she knew the difference between coaching and therapy, she shrugged her shoulders, uncertain like the loose, undefined gray color of her clothes.

I discussed with Carrie that coaching is distinct from therapy, with completely different expectations and goals. To get the desired results, it is necessary to commit to the coaching program and follow up with a task for each session. In coaching, no diagnosis would be involved and no treatment plan would be provided. We would not dig into the past: the focus would be on moving forward and bringing her into the most resourceful state possible. This would be done using only Neuro-Linguistic Programming techniques and models, which are different from psychotherapy. Carrie signed the agreement for the coaching program and was ready to dive in.

For those of you who have obtained the most success from coaching sessions, you may know that the magic happens when the right coach shows up at the right time and helps to transform a limited mindset using the power of your mind intentionally and skillfully. The art of coaching includes mastery and virtuosity to help people get to their highest potential, which is called the "Best Version of Yourself."

Carrie and I started working on her goals so she could "fly" symbolically and literally to where she wanted to be, instead of being stuck. No one's goal is big or small. It depends on the person and circumstances, as it was for Carrie. Her short-term goals were clearly defined, and she wanted to feel unstuck in her choices. She wanted to run her marathon and thus desired to be motivated to run every day. Her biggest dream was to feel freedom and fly over Rio De Janeiro. But to travel to Brazil seemed impossible with her old mindset and where she was currently in her life and work.

We collaborated and both worked hard. I provided her with the best result-producing techniques I knew, and she did everything that needed to be done, including the tasking, the exercising, the practices, etc. We would meet weekly for two-hour sessions, learn about her strategies and painful stuck states, discover how she thought, and how we could change her thoughts, and, most importantly, her beliefs.

Over time I noticed that Carrie was beginning to walk more lively and energetically. The life force would start flowing through the movements of her legs, making her feel "more grounded and strong," as she said. She also chose to wear blue instead of gray now. Blue was her favorite color, the "color of the blue ocean," she said. The compass of her mindset slowly began to change direction.

During one session, while we talked about her progress, I mentioned to her:

"Do you know that the name Carrie means 'free'? Or 'being free'!?"

Her green eyes sparkled like two precious emeralds fired with passion and lifeforce. She replied: "No! This is the first time I have heard that. How funny that I've felt the opposite most of my life: I've felt stuck at work, and with my relationships, coping with the stress through so much coffee."

Carrie had her hope ignited by the progress she was making. She came to one of her following sessions and said:

"I was driving the car the other day and the song came on the radio: '*I believe I can fly... I believe I can touch the sky. I think about it night and day, spread my wings and fly away.*' I started to cry because I could not believe it. I realized that I did not believe in myself..."

I mentioned to her that synchronicities were starting to occur in her life. According to C. G. Jung, we are on the right path when such a process happens to us. Synchronicities can happen anytime, and we have to be open to them. For example, you could hear the answer to your question from someone standing next to you in line or, like Carrie did, on the radio. Be aware, and pay attention. The universe is "always talking" to us with signs and symbols in our dreams and meditations as well.

"Does these signs mean I'm on the right track with my mindset?" Carrie asked.

"Exactly," I confirmed.

Carrie listed her goals, dream travel destinations, and "What Makes Me Feel Good" items so she could have a "go-to" when she found herself stressed while performing at her job. She was rereading her list of goals twice a day - thirty minutes before going to sleep, and right after waking up – to set her mindset in the right direction with what she wanted, and not with what the media or TV news segment were offering. As a result, she was more in control of what she wanted to stream to her mind. During sessions we practiced the S.M.A.R.T. goal model used in NLP coaching when setting goals. She was "getting there," as she'd said about her progress.

One day, she brought her Vision Board. I could see that the pictures were neatly cut out, carefully arranged, and glued to the cardboard. Her two dogs were there, and she was running a marathon. Also on the board were images of her healthy food plates and green salads, as well as the word "success" and the phrase: "Yes! I can do it!" She also included a bird's-eye-view picture of Rio de Janeiro. The beautiful blue water sparkled, like her emerald eyes did when she thought of gliding over the magnificent Jesus Statue and lush green mountains. Of course, she'd also put on the board the song lyrics by R. Kelly, *"I believe I can fly, cause I believe in ME…»*

We looked at the Vision Board pictures and discussed if they gave her a boost of energy and made her move forward in life. I saw that Carrie was so inspired to work on that Vision Board. She even hang it where it could be the first thing she saw in the morning, and the last thing she saw before she closed her eyes. She was about to gain momentum in life…

PART TWO: HOW TO FOCUS ON WHAT YOU WANT

Discovering new choices, opportunities and a new Carrie

"I can't come tomorrow for the session," Carrie cried over the phone. "I injured my knee yesterday when I was running."

"I'm so sorry to hear that," I said. "Have you been helped?"

"Yes. I can walk but not run and cannot go for long distances and it's hard to drive."

"Good. Would you consider a Zoom session instead? And you can tell me what happened," I replied.

"That will work, I guess. I'm still going to be at home." It sounded as though Carrie was questioning if she still wanted to cancel her session… "*What kind of resistance do I have? And why?*" These questions were running through her head, as Carrie later shared.

We decided to schedule the Zoom session. As it started, Carrie said excitedly, "I was doing so well! I cut down my coffee in half! And I was so happy."

"How did you do that?" I exclaimed.

"I used the technique you taught me before. I listed all the benefits that I would get when I cut down on coffee and substitute it with healthier drinks. I did the same for my running training, even though I would be driving back home from work. I was reminding myself about the benefits of exercise and running."

"Hey Carrie, this is very impressive!" I said supporting her.

"I usually run by myself. Sometimes my boyfriend will join me. He used to go to the gym while I was running, but now he feels much better around me. He even mentioned that I had changed. He noticed my eyes sparkling when I shared my Vision Board and Bucket List with him."

"Great job, Carrie!" I said validating her choices.

"The 'reframing' I've learned from our sessions has worked like a charm: I even taught the technique to my boyfriend. I no longer need to say to myself in the morning that I *need* to run. I'm saying I *choose* to do it, and that I'll be able to run the marathon from San

Diego upon the PCH towards Big Sur… Even though I know it's an ambition, I am working every day on it. But everything is gone now that I've injured my knee," Carrie continued. "My motivation is gone, and I'm off the schedule with my training sessions. My dog's condition worsened the same day as my injury and I could not take him to the vet, so I had to ask my boyfriend to do it, causing him to have to take time from work. I felt so bad asking him to do that for me. I am such a mess!" she said crying.

"OK," I said. "Remember the rubber band? Does that take you out of spiraling down with your negative thoughts?"

"Yes."

"Good. Now, how would you reframe your current state of being overwhelmed?"

"I guess there is time to slow down and process things and reflect," Carrie said slowly, drying her tears.

"That's right! It's time to practice what you've learned about using the right mindset."

"I guess so!"

"In other words, is there an opportunity for you to make a breakthrough in your thought process and master your mindset while your body is taking a break, isn't it?"

"Right," Carrie said. "I can see it now."

"What is one step you could do today that will bring you closer towards your goals?" I asked her, catching a good moment to make her focus on what she wanted and create a positive statement.

"I can continue to visualize that I'm healed and running again, and can see myself participating in a marathon."

"Good! Now when you see yourself running the marathon completely healed and healthy, do you see yourself from above or through your own eyes?"

"I see myself from above," Carrie said.

"Good! Now I want you to see yourself running the marathon through your own eyes," I said. "Feel it and hear the sound of people around you. Make the image colorful and attune brightness to it, like on the screen of your iPhone. Make the sound in this movie louder and make it more vibrant. Feel your legs running strongly and your lungs breathing in and out freely. Do you see it? Feel it? Hear it?"

"Yes!"

"Now, make it even more vivid and notice what's changed."

"I'm in the process. I am living it!" Carrie exclaimed.

"Beautiful! Practice this attunement of your sensory modalities - visual, kinesthetic, auditorial - till the next session."

At the end, we did the "Like to Dislike" exercise, which is very popular in NLP coaching when a person wants to stop eating a particular food. In Carrie's case, she wanted to let go of coffee, and she did! She became free in her food choices and was no longer a victim of her old habits.

As we continued the coaching program, we covered what happens when our unconscious mind gets out of its comfort zone and impedes us out of fear of success. Like a computer program that is running in the background, our unconscious mind says: "You are in this state of homeostasis, but even if you try to make an effort, I'll bring you back down to where it's known, and familiar, and not necessarily pleasant." That's why Carrie had resistance to change at some point during the transformational process. How do we change this?

Our breakthroughs come when we recognize our stuck states, set our mindset in the right direction, make an effort, and keep going until new thinking or behavior becomes our everyday habitual way of living, our 'new' homeostasis. For those changes to take place, we need courage and perseverance, don't we?

The winning part of Carrie's character was that she would show up at each coaching session with the assigned task completed meticulously. She was craving changes in her life, not the coffee anymore. She had been stuck in her limited thinking and needed a breakthrough, as the old self, old strategies and beliefs, the old mindset were not working anymore. She was discovering her new approach to life, new empowering beliefs and values, and of course learned self-love practices. Additionally, she was beginning to accept help from others. She was discovering a new version of herself – a New Carrie.

PART THREE: LIVE YOUR POWER WITH A NEW MINDSET

Magnificent emerald ring

Carrie showed up to the session in a beautiful silk blouse with green, blue and turquoise colors. In an energetic, almost dancing manner, she reflected with a big smile that her sparkly "inner waters" were clear and calm, and that her "inner sky" would ask for its gliding… We had done the "internal cleaning process," and gray clouds were disappearing from Carrie's horizon as more clarity and confidence showed up in her – which were reflected in the external events of her life.

"I went to an interview this week for a new job!" declared Carrie right at the beginning of the session.

"Yes! This deserves celebration and acknowledgment. Reward yourself for each success, no matter how small or big! Your mind needs this confirmation!" I matched her in her happy and exciting voice.

"Most likely, I will get the job," Carrie said. "So I can save up some money for my trip to Brazil."

"Wonderful!"

"And I found a school where I can learn hang gliding!"

"Yes!"

"I no longer need coffee to energize myself," she continued.

I noticed that lately she was filling the sessions describing her new choices and changes, rather than me pouring into her.

"When I was driving here, I had all green lights on the road. So I guess it's a good sign," Carrie continued verbalizing her thoughts.

"Yes. Absolutely! Now, are you ready for another challenge?" I asked to check how strongly planted she was in her new mindset.

"Yes!" she said.

"OK! Now you know about the synchronicities you just experienced while you were driving today to the session. Write these occurrences in your journal for two weeks, next to your gratitude list. Then, focus on what you want to use your new mindset intentionally. Finally, let your unconscious mind know that you notice its symbolic language by keeping the record of your dreams and practicing your new behavior and new choices."

"Deal!" Carrie shined her beautiful smile.

"OK. Great. Now, would you like to seal your deal with the most powerful anchoring technique that will be available to you all the time?"

"Of course!" she readily replied.

I explained the exercise called "The Ring of Power," which involved a concept of anchoring. At the end I asked her to imagine a circle in front of her, one colored shiny emerald green – her favorite color – just like the color of the emerald ring on her finger. Then, I instructed her to "step" into the imaginary "Ring of Power." As she did so, her face and whole body beamed with the energizing wave of the renewed life force energy, which ran through her like a current of electricity. She was ecstatic, energized, motivated, passionate and powerful.

"If I just believe it, there is nothing to it..." those lyrics were in my mind while I observed Carrie "anchoring" the powerful state into her full body, into every cell, into her being. Shining her light, Carrie was filling herself with nothing but strength, confidence and power. We "anchored" these states to her emerald ring, so now she had a tangible, visual representation of her new powerful mindset.

With the incident of her knee injury, her body had shown and wisely "taught" her that there was time for stillness in her life and time for action. There was time to "breathe in" and "breathe out." While healing her knee, Carrie learned flexibility in her thought process and relationships. She communicated and treated herself differently with love and respect, and asked for help when needed. I was in awe as I witnessed her transformation and breakthrough, a poignant reminder of the power of our mind.

We scheduled a follow-up session two weeks later, and then a month later, so she could have time to practice living her new choices and behaviors.

During the two week follow-up session, Carrie shared that she was adjusting to her new job and getting to know her coworkers. She'd replied yes to a work email invitation to run for her company's half-marathon event. Before, she would never have been able to do that – she would have shied away from any challenge and gone with the flow, even if it didn't serve her, or if her gut feeling and intuition knew that hiking group could go in the wrong direction. She had now learned how to trust herself and her internal voice, and how to become true to herself, provide love and respect to herself. The results of this new mindset could be seen in the outside world. She was living her life with the power of the "green light" of the emerald ring that she anchored in her mind and body.

A few months later, I got a short letter from Carrie with a small picture of her in a beautiful, bright, flowery tropical dress with shiny green and blue colors.

"My dog passed away a few weeks ago," she wrote, "but beforehand, I created an album about my best times with my dog, and celebrated his 12th birthday with my friends and family. I focus now on the love that I had for him, knowing that he had his own time and I provided the best care he deserved. I'm leaving behind, with love and gratitude, what has been dear to me – my memories – and I'm keeping what I need: love, lessons and wisdom.

P.S. My boyfriend got a job in Rio and I'm flying there to see him in a couple of weeks!"

"I am flying!" Carrie screamed out of happiness, while she flew over Rio, knowing that she was in constant creation of her life. By then, she knew that whatever she focused her mindset towards, she could achieve! She discovered the magic inside her mind. She saw everything from a bird's eye view: her past problems and challenges as the roads in her life streamed together like the streaming rivers she saw below. The memories intertwined like the silver lining thread that is woven into our colorful tapestry of life with its ups and downs, success and growth, tears of grief and tears of happiness.

Carrie circled over the valley. The color of the emerald ring that she wore during the first session on her finger perfectly matched the greenery of nature in Brazil. Carrie was free from fear and pain, and enjoyed her freedom and power! She knew she was living her Best Version of Herself! Her victory in discovering mastery over her mindset was celebrated at full speed.

The next week, I got a call:

"Are you the one who does the Breakthrough Sessions?"

"Yes, I am," I said.

"I am a friend of Carrie," the woman said. "I could not believe that such a drastic transformation was possible for her. I want that too."

I smiled and answered: "Yes. If you are ready for change and to elevate your mindset…"

"I can't live in pain anymore," the person confided.

"When can you come for your first Goal Setting Session?"

*"I believe I can fly, I believe I can touch the sky." Because I believe in YOU…*those words flew through my mind as I remembered Carrie's song. I knew that if I believed in my clients' potential to change, they would believe in it too, and they would have the opportunity to turn their lives around through the power of their mindset.

"Transform and master your mindset and you will transform and master your life."

~ Gary A. Ferraro

CHAPTER FOUR

Never Underestimate the Power Within

By Amanda Lees

I sat with swollen eyes from the tears that were falling. I felt so inadequate as a human. I thought I had failed my children, my husband, and all those around me. I had once been confident in all my roles, but now I felt lost and alone. I cried ugly tears. You know the ones when you cannot stop the stream of tears and the snorting - and don't forget the snot. I was glad to be alone so no one could see me. After this extended session of ugly crying I realized that my mindset was the one thing I did have control over. I needed to use this to pull me from the black hole. I started that day, but I am still mastering my mindset a decade down the track. It is a constant journey that I continue to learn to master every day.

I had driven away from my home. I needed to escape. That day was my thirty-second birthday. For just one day, I wanted to pretend my life was not my reality. Even on my birthday, the facts were staring me in the face. I could not change these facts, but I could change my mindset. At this point in my life, when I felt lost and alone, I dug deeper than ever to take control of my mindset. It was powerful.

I left my home that day feeling angry. I was frustrated and exhausted. I felt resentful that my kids could not hold it together for just one day. I now realize how unrealistic that expectation was. They were not trying to piss me off. They were not trying to ruin my day. The truth was, just like me, they were trying to do their best.

I knew I would not solve all my problems in one day. But I did find peace and acceptance with what I was facing. I found peace with not knowing *how* to get out of this black hole but knowing I would. This time would pass. I had finally accepted where I was in my life. This was the beginning of mastering my mindset. Acceptance is often the hardest. True acceptance of the situation to own your story. How can you move forward if you do not acknowledge where you are now?

I had ticked the boxes of all the accomplishments I wanted to achieve by this time in my life. I had completed my studies as a registered nurse with a post-graduate diploma in women's health. I had married my childhood sweetheart, whom I loved and adored. And together we had three amazing children and a beautiful home to raise them in. So why would I want to escape?

We had been thrown many obstacles along our short journey into parenthood. Yet, I remained positive and could always pick myself up and keep moving forward. But this was becoming harder and harder to do. We had three complicated pregnancies, with our daughter arriving at 31 weeks, our son trying to enter the world at 29 weeks, and our youngest son entering at 35 weeks, complete with a hole in his heart. In addition, we had faced uncontrolled asthma, chronic pneumonia, meningitis, severe speech disorders, and anaphylaxis allergies to multiple foods, to name a few of the challenges along the way. Yet, we had navigated our way through these challenges and my husband, Scotty, and I were proud of our resilience through these times.

But over the last 12 months, we had fallen into an almighty black hole, and I was struggling to see any light.

My daughter had been diagnosed with Asperger's Syndrome, now identified as Autism Spectrum Disorder (ASD) and generalized anxiety. She was only six. My son was also diagnosed with ASD, generalized anxiety, and severe phonological speech disorder.

He was only five. We had completely lost our daughter and she was out of control. Extroverted in her coping mechanisms, she left holes in our walls when she could not control her emotions. Our son had become introverted with his coping mechanisms, which was just as scary. We found our five-year-old son scratching himself out of photos as he thought it would be best if he were not here. Nothing could have prepared me for what our family was currently facing.

Mastering your mindset is not something you wake up and turn on, like flicking a switch. *Just be positive. Tell yourself everything is great. Find the good in every situation.* That is just not reality. Mastering your mindset takes time, practice, and patience. I had days when I did not want to get out of bed. Days that I did not recognize my life. Days when I wondered how I got here. I have also had days that made me jump out of bed filled with excitement about what was ahead, and days that I never wanted to end as they were just so amazing. Your mindset is vital through all these days. The good, the bad, and all the days in between.

For me, the first step to mastering my mindset was finding one thing at the beginning of each day to be grateful for. On my thirty second birthday, I was grateful for the sanctuary of my car. On other days I am thankful for a particular person in my life or an achievement of one of my children. Some days I am just grateful for coffee to help me get through another day. I found that it did not need to be of great significance, but to start the day with a positive thought sets the mind for the rest of the day. This was something that I also needed to be consistent with. So, every morning I would write down one thing I was grateful for.

I also changed my thought process around different situations that gave me *so* much frustration. For example, the first week back to school. For my two older children, this was especially difficult. Their anxiety would build leading up to the return to school. By the time the first day back would arrive, they would be nauseated (at times, my daughter would vomit), clothes became uncomfortable due to heightened sensitivities, and they were unable to eat. They would be irritable and agitated. Getting them dressed and out the door was like going to war.

When it was time to pick them up and they were in the comfort of our car or our home, all hell would break loose. Hayden would soil himself (even though he had been toilet trained for years) and the tears would follow. Emily would yell in frustration from her day but could not tell me what was upsetting her. I would do my best to comfort them both. But, inside, I was frustrated and disappointed at how hard school was for them. Questioning why they could not go to school and be happy like all the other kids. (As if all the other kids had no problems!) I would tell myself that all the therapies we had taken them to and the money we had spent had been a waste of time and that this would be my life forever. These thoughts had to change.

I had to lead by example, not only with my actions but with my thoughts as well. First, I would acknowledge how hard the first week back to school was for them. I would tell them I knew how hard it was for them. I would also praise them and tell them how proud I was because I knew they had tried their best. I would tell them they had everything they needed to get through this week. I changed my expectations, my attitude, and my actions. I built them up to know they could get through this. Because they could, they always did. When I picked them up, I would shower them with praise. Congratulating them that they made it through another day. If they did not make it through the whole day because it was too overwhelming, I would commend them for going to school and trying their best, despite how hard they knew it would be.

I would take the first week off work, so I was not rushed. I would be calm and ensure I was not adding to their anxiety. I would collect them from school and debrief with them when the day ended. I made dinners I knew they liked and had a good snack for them when they arrived home. I ensured I was available for them and set them up to succeed. I also set examples with my actions. I would soak in the bath with Epsom salts when we had a bad day. I would let the kids know that I needed some downtime. And they all now love a bath as much as me. I ensure I go to bed early if I have a big day ahead and I let them know why I am doing this. They know that sleep is important and affects how you feel the next day. I practice yoga. Some of my favorite classes were when Josh and I would go together before he started school and he would join in. I make time to be with Scotty and with my friends. As much as I am there for my children, I also need them to know I need time to be me. When I take care of myself I am a better human, and that benefits everyone.

It was around this time that I also reached out to a psychologist. Something I never thought I would do for myself. I had seen several psychologists to support the kids, but what about me? What made me think that through these rough seas, I was invincible? I needed the skills to keep me afloat for myself so that I could support my children. This was invaluable. I had someone looking out for me and I was given strategies to help me cope. This not only benefited me and everyone around me, but I began to see an obvious pattern. I needed to take care of myself.

With the positive changes in our lives, we were starting to see glimmers of light. Moments that gave us joy. Days that were not so hard. In these times, I still needed to master my mindset. I needed to acknowledge these days as much as I did the more challenging days. Over time I have become better at this. I can now soak up the good days and use them to fuel my soul. To appreciate the day for what it is.

When we first had these good days, I was fearful that they would not last. I was waiting for the next bad day. This had to change. I slowly released my fear of the past. I had to acknowledge that it was, in fact, the past not the present. Several sessions with my psychologist allowed me to let go of the past. She noticed this fear in me and made me return to that fear. It was hard. She made me talk about it in detail and process it. Cue more ugly tears as she guided me through my feelings; I will always be grateful for that process. I truly released the past and could move forward more freely.

Over the last decade, I have had dark days. Fast forward seven years from that day in my car and once again -this time in the shower - my eyes were puffy, and I was in disbelief at where I was in my life. This time my son was not scratching himself out of the photo but taking action to kill himself. He was 11. I had feelings once again of anger, resentment, and pure frustration. But they came and they left me much faster than before. I acknowledged the situation and knew we had everything we needed to get through this. I knew Hayden was trying his best. I also knew we needed to take more action to help him. I frequently use one statement with myself and my children: "Every problem has a solution; this time will pass." Some solutions are harder to find and take more effort. We had reached a crossroad in life and if we continued down the same path, we would continue to walk in darkness.

Every day we have choices. So many choices. The hard choices we make often have the biggest rewards. Despite our positive mindset and using the many strategies we had learned along the way, we needed to acknowledge our situation. At this point in my life, our whole family struggled to be happy. The hard times outweighed our good. It had crept up on us over time, but it was now staring us in the face. We went against the grain of society and down the path less traveled.

Together with my husband, we planned to pack up our home, take twelve months leave from work, and travel around Australia in a caravan and focus on our family. It was amazing. We did not panic and leave. Instead, we chose to make a change. It took about nine months to plan. All our healthcare team supported us and that change of direction saved our family. It also injected new life into us and a passion for living. It was one of the hardest but most rewarding choices which continues to benefit us even now that we are settled again into work and school.

We left our home on the twelfths of January 2020. We went with open minds and had no idea what the next twelve months would bring. We all know now that it brought a global pandemic as COVID-19 swept through the world like wildfire. When COVID-19 hit Australia, we were in Victoria. Being a nurse and having the inside information from my work, we knew our plans would be affected. And they were. Over the years, Scotty and I had learned how to ride the unpredictable wave of life. This sudden change did not rock us. We were disappointed and we needed to come up with a solution. We acknowledged, accepted, and adapted. We focused on our goal for that year. We were taking time to be with our family. We both knew we did not want to return home. 'Every problem has a solution. This time will pass.'

We bolted to South Australia the night before all internal borders closed in Australia. We bunkered down in a caravan park until we had permission to leave. We received calls from family and friends who were disappointed for us. But we had a new plan. Yes, we had not planned for this pandemic, but we were still together as a family. We had no alarms, work, or mainstream school, and we were all together. We were loving life. We embraced every day and made the most out of our time together. Lockdown in South Australia was only six weeks, and we were back on the road, free to roam South Australia. By July, we also had access to the Northern Territory and were in Western Australia by September. I had the best year of my life.

When we returned home on my fortieth birthday, twelve months later, my mindset was stronger than ever. That year on the road gave me the time to reflect on my journey. When I was a girl, I wanted to be a mum and get happily married. I have achieved this.

The journey I have walked along the way was one I could never have imagined. Like so many people, I have had moments where my life is far from what I ever dreamed. I have wondered how I got here and how I would get through these times.

The challenges I have faced and obstacles I have overcome I shared in my memoir *According to Plan: Riding the Unpredictable Waves of Motherhood.* I began to write in 2020 and it has allowed me to heal in ways I never knew were possible. It allowed me to reflect, acknowledge, and be proud of my journey. I continued to write when we returned home, and it became clear that I wanted to share my story. The act of writing had already exceeded my expectations in helping me to heal. I was willing to share if I could inspire others with my story. Before I knew it, I had a manuscript. For a girl who struggled to read and write, I had now written a book that I was extremely proud of.

Traveling around Australia in a caravan is not the answer for everyone. That was just the answer for us. Life is about finding what works for you and listening to your inner voice—standing up for yourself and doing what is right. Taking care of yourself can be perceived as selfish, but it could not be further from the truth. When you value yourself and care for yourself, you create the best version of yourself. That enables you to be the best partner, friend, sibling, mother, and so on. By honoring yourself, you honor everyone around you.

As I write, this week is my boys' first week back at school. It went so smoothly. It has now become such a habit of praise and acknowledgment. We still acknowledge that this week will be challenging, but they know they have everything to get through. They now have more ease and confidence, which comes with time and a positive mindset. We still celebrate every Friday that we have made it through another week. We celebrate the small wins. So many small wins make great lives.

It has taken time to master my mindset. It constantly evolves as I grow. It has not happened overnight or over a week or even a year. It is a work in progress. One that I need to monitor constantly. To assess what is working and what is not—asking if I am being true to myself, to my inner voice. It also needs to be nurtured and surrounded by people who will encourage me on my journey. I am mindful of who I give my time—acknowledging who makes me feel good about myself and who brings me down. As a result, I have more joy in my life and allow myself to truly enjoy these moments. I will still have hard days, but I have everything I need to keep moving forward.

We all have our moments, and despite what our minds tell us, we all have what we need to get through these challenging days. We are unstoppable when we use our minds to empower and not restrain us. This takes time, consistency, and patience. Above all, be kind to yourself.

“Happiness has to do with your mindset, not with outside circumstance.”

~Steve Maraboli

CHAPTER FIVE

Soul Mastery

Luxury in Harmony with Nature

By Inarra Aryane Griffyn

My name is Inarra Aryane Griffyn, and I teach the mastery that is found in nature. Inarra means "Shining Light," a name that chose me when I chose the path of mastery.

When teaching the mastery of nature, we are dealing with a contradiction. Nature doesn't have a mindset. Yet, I work with entrepreneurs to teach them about the mastery of nature. To move into this realm, we must dispel the word "mindset" and improve it, transform it, and experience it. But this is not done with the mind. Instead, it is done with two threads of consciousness; one the masculine, mastery, and the other the feminine, mystery. The mindset I refer to involves a practical application of knowledge to achieve skill while surrendering to the mystery of your soul's calling.

Nature as a teacher is, first and foremost, a teacher of cycles. This is the deepest teaching, irrefutable in its simplicity. By allowing the path of nature, which is successful in every endeavor, we see the wisdom of working in cycles, and for that, the first step is you have to know where you are right now in the cycle of your mastery.

Mindset Lesson 1 is to assess where you are on your journey.

Ask yourself, where are you? At the beginning of a new path? In the middle, perhaps bogged down in routine? Or are you at the golden stage of mastery which is a stage of bearing fruit in a cycle? You could also be in the death cycle. Is something ending? Be clear and honest about how you answer your question.

My own experience on my path to mastery mindset started at the age of nine. Standing in Grandmother's garden in North Yorkshire, I realized I was part of a vast connected Oneness. Teachings were being downloaded into my young mind and when I attempted to explain this to Grandma Ida, she then spoke to me of Healers, called Witches, who danced naked on the moors and healed people with milk. So I set out to find these wild Nature Healers. It was not until my 20s that I met them. I made a long journey to find them. Living in Canada, as my parents had emigrated there, I felt this was not my land. However, it was a recurring thought and I trusted my instinct. So after finishing University, without making a specific plan, I traveled across Europe, arriving in London knowing only one acquaintance, and never returned.

Lesson 2: Be prepared to travel far away from home. When you hear the call, go.

You must learn to trust yourself first to connect with your true calling. How do you trust? You learn to tap into your feelings so that if something feels off, don't do it. It's simple.

Lesson 3: Trust your instincts.

Instinct is one of the key ingredients to mastery. Therefore, we have to find a way to cultivate it. I stumbled upon all the ingredients of a Mastery Mindset, living my life fully. I lived mastery as I learned how an apprentice does and then put the recipe together to help my clients. Leaving Canada to move to England was the first big lesson about trust.

We must surrender to trust beyond the logical circumstances of our lives. David Bowie once said, "If you feel safe in the area you're working in, you're not working in the right area. So always go a little further into the water than you feel you're capable of being in. Go a little out of your depth, and when you don't feel that your feet are quite touching the bottom, you're just about in the right place to do something exciting."

Lesson 4: Stay out of your comfort zone.

There were threads of the mystery unraveling at that time. I was courageous, leaving everything behind to follow my soul's path. Although it was a challenging and exciting experience meeting those Healers who worked with the Seasons, Cycles of the Moon, and Ancient Festivals, it felt like I came home. I learned everything I could about perfect timing and how to become in tune with nature.

The right timing, as you are manifesting, means some alignments work as anchors to make sure the seed grows. It's obvious when you think about gardening. Planting a seed in mid-winter won't work. So it's about tapping into the layers of all the cycles you are playing with. It's about slowing down, taking a moment and a breath to discern where you are on the cycle. Then it's a matter of asking what you are growing and letting go of, respectively. What needs to go so that something else can flourish? For instance, what thoughts need to go? If I'm holding onto the idea of "it's hard to make money," then making money will be hard. How do we replace old thoughts continuously so that the nourishment of all new ideas becomes available? The answer is being clear about where you are going.

London in the 80s was music, art, sensory stimulation, and cool vibes and I thrived. I worked as a photographer daily and studied ritual, ceremony, and energy healing in the evening. I had a job, but more than that, I regarded myself as a Healer. It began as a feeling. I then declared it. "I want to be a great healer," I announced to the universe. Shortly after, I was diagnosed with a terminal illness. In between my declaration and my dance with death, there was a steady voice saying, "That is not your story. You're going to be okay." A surge of energy bit at my heels, speeding up the journey. A lot was at stake—my life.

Lesson 5: Make choices as if it is your last day.

At that point, I chose a lifestyle to support well-being and health as a priority. I formulated the best principles for a happy life.

On a trip to India, I walked up a mountain and meditated on a sacred shrine. Just like when I was nine, something opened up and I experienced a direct Divine Connection. A download began. "Happiness is a choice." And then, "You'll never be happy doing 9 to 5." I went up the mountain in one state of being, and then irrevocably, alchemically, I came down utterly changed. Happiness had occurred to me: some people were happy and others weren't. I never imagined that it was a choice.

The depth of this realization made me a different person and I chose happiness.

The formula was simple. Choose the non-negotiable ingredients in a day, as if it is your last day on Earth, that make you happy. This formula is the beginning of a mastery blueprint and you can create one just like this. Ask yourself, on a perfect day, what would you be doing?

Mine went like this:

- yoga
- cappuccino
- nature
- sensuality
- music
- creativity
- connection with people
- ritual
- animals

It started as a simple list that would work whether I had a little or a lot of money.

Notice that there was no "work" associated with my life. Instead, it was creativity. I created a day that would stand as the best day ever, with a recipe I could savor for the whole of my life. Cappuccino has since been replaced with a matcha latte, and it's not just the pleasure of the taste. It's what it represents: ME TIME. I've never been a homebody. Seeking activity hubs near home keeps me interested in life. The buzz of a great coffee shop with conversation and interaction is what it's all about for me.

Align with the feeling of happiness and ask yourself what makes you happy every day and do it.

Lesson 6: Choose what makes you happy.

I refined the list to be one of my core values and pleasures. Values are the most profound ingredient on any list and form the ethical agreements in your world and your boundaries. The map of your most pleasurable ingredients becomes a map of your most successful life. If you leave out any elements, resistance and contraction show up.

I was not one to choose a primary focus but defined myself as moving in time with the cycles of incoming and outgoing visions. By the time I'd been a professional photographer for 20 years, writing books and running retreats in the UK themed with yoga, meditation, and ceremonies at sacred sites, I felt a vigorous stir in my heart. That's the best way to describe it. I'd been happily working and bringing all these ingredients into my life and suddenly, I felt another priority, money. I'd never been interested in money but noticed in my profession the limits to how much I could make doing a non-commercial style of photography. London was an expensive place to live, and I understood that lifestyle required money. This caused a shift in my alignment from being enough to wanting more than enough.

Lesson 7: To move into abundance, you have to feel good enough in yourself, experience gratitude and then desire more. There's nothing wrong with you wanting more. It's like turning on a tap.

One Christmas Eve, as I looked over the River Thames in London, I strongly wanted to speak directly to the Universe. So I spoke out loud, "that's it. After the holidays, I'm never returning to my photography job and will find something else that gives me pleasure and money." I was at the height of my career, standing in a James Bond-style flat after photographing interiors, and I knew none of my friends or family would understand this choice. On the outside, it looked as if I'd made it. But I knew there was more and I was going for a Quantum Shift.

How do you do that?

Lesson 8: Shut off all exits, so there is no back door, and follow the unknown path. This is the condition of opportunity.

A few days later, I received an email. The header asked, "Do you want to change your life?" I felt a pulse go through me. "Yes, I do, but I have no idea how."

A call was set up with a group called The Enlightened Millionaire Institute, and I trusted the coach from how I felt during the first call. I noticed I felt safe and confident, and a warm feeling flowed through my body. Even though I was asked to pay $6,000, which I didn't have, when he suggested I use a credit card, I felt sure enough to see it as a way forward, enabling me to pay back in installments. Calculated risk is one of the entrepreneurs' top personality traits, and I chose YES without knowing how. Three months into the training, my homework was to go and buy a property. It was an outrageously bold proposition.

Lesson 9: If you feel yes, say yes and then figure it out.

My coach reassured me, "You've studied the figures. You know the type of property you're working with, so now it's time for action!" So I bought my second property, launching a property development company in London that, 12 years later, was worth ten million US dollars. This milestone allowed me to reflect on the qualities of a mastery mindset that took me that far.

Trust, calculated risk, feeling the flow of alignment while out of my comfort zone, and sticking to my list of happiness.

In that phase of life, I followed my instinct to plant a seed that grew into property development. Then, with the unexpected world economic crisis of 2008, I used my mastery mindset to change rather than staying in property to move into the next cycle. I turned to my spiritual roots and mixed them, finance and business. It was time for me to go public with my real healing work.

I had learned to achieve a life of luxury and I wanted to teach others how to reach it with strong conscious foundations: luxury in harmony with nature. From then on, I wove in threads of wealth, abundance, and luxury with spiritual and ethical values. Luxury is the pleasure principle and when people experience pleasure, they are in RECEIVING MODE. That's the Feminine way. So my work had to include the Divine Feminine, PAUSE, to sustain the Divine Masculine, PUSH.

To grow and manifest a vision, there is a time to create the environment in which a seed is planted, a time to expand, and a time to withdraw and marinate. Each stage supports the other. It is a harmony of Masculine and Feminine blueprints. Do one without the other and you get burnout or weak energy lines that break at the first sign of stress. Solid growth in the quantum realm requires a steady stream of planting and space for the next shoot to emerge.

Many years later, during a plant medicine ceremony, I heard a voice asking me, "Are you willing to work with the super-rich?" I can't say that this was ever a fantasy of mine, but at that moment, I knew it was an important spiritual question being asked by God herself. And I breathed and paused and then said, "YES!"

Lesson 10: Listen to your inner guidance. Listen to Source.

Something happened after that ceremony. I first read an article about a billionaire who had paid to shoot one of the last black rhinos dead. It was sickening. Then I read another article about a billionaire buying up vast areas of nature and turning its guardianship over to Indigenous peoples. By the time he dies, he will have bought up 15% of global land and may achieve 20%. Again, the spiritual connection was illuminated.

My vision became clear: I am to work with two kinds of entrepreneurs as I weave the spiritual threads of two polarities.

1. **Spiritual People with conscious businesses who shy away from money and help them raise their game financially.**
2. **More traditional businesses to help them incorporate spiritual values to make them ethical, conscious, and sustainable.**

My job was to work with entrepreneurs to shift the money balance into the hands of conscious New Earth influencers and visionaries, to get money into the hands of healers and help the planet, people and animals. This was my moment of stepping into soul mastery. I found my calling by surrendering to the mysteries and honing my skills in mastery.

Mastery does not occur early in the journey but at a time when the apprentice has learned how to apply the tools of manifestation to their vision. They are not beginners. Instead, they have worked with their knowledge and even failed.

To reframe failure here, it's not something you experience because, from the eyes of a master, it is simply a path not taken.

Lesson 11: There is no failure, only a path not taken.

In Medieval times when a young child had to learn a skill that would support the family for life, there were three stages to the learning; the apprentice (14-21 years), the Journey Man (21-28) and finally becoming a Master Craftsperson. The same is true of a Shaman/ Medicine Woman/ Healer in the magical, ritual realm. The apprentice would learn herbal lore, energy work, and ceremonies early on with a magical tutor. Once the connection and skills were established, there were rituals of commitment to the path and the teacher. These came in the form of initiations and practices, such as vision quests. This period in magical training was honing the craft while governed by the rules of the master and being held accountable.

When it was time to take their place as Healers in their own right, the initiations at the next level often included death/ rebirth rites. Sexuality, ingestion of semi-poisonous substances, and psychedelics to induce a death state were also part of the experience. The initiate's agreement was becoming of service to the land and its people while in skilled stone masonry, the Journeyman would have to produce a work of art and be tested by the guild to be sure they were up to the name of the master. Both paths show us how we are trained to be ready for our maximum expression of the skills of the trade and surrender to the calling.

So how does this relate to mastery in business?

To create magnificent feats of building, business, and art, we must experience it as if our creations are essential and non-negotiable, as if the mere fact of them not coming to life would be a loss. Therefore, going to the highest level of consciousness, worthy of our abilities, is vital. It's likened to a life-or-death experience.

Lesson 12: Your work, art, and projects are essential to you being you. Put you first.

In other words, not fully expressing your creativity is not an option when you are in a mastery mindset. It's like living a half-life. You can feel the future impact of not fulfilling your dreams or legacy in the present. This lights a fire in your belly. Nature expresses this elegantly. A tree must be a tree. A panther must be a panther. You must be you.

We have this life, our opportunity to fulfill our dreams, so not living it to the fullest is a kind of death and would leave us with regrets. That's living at the edge of mastery.

I now teach the art of soul mastery. For example, I use soul mastery techniques to train my clients to be the kings and queens in my 11 Queens 11 Kings Mastery Program. 11 is the number of mastery in numerology. In harnessing the power of mastery and mystery, they break through to the level of visionary leaders in their chosen field.

A suggestion:

Taking your core values and pleasures, list what they are. Order your day according to exactly when and what you prefer: when to exercise, when you are most creative, when to make time for pleasure, and what is that pleasure? Make them non-negotiable. Shut the back door to any other excuses for creating your best life. Prioritize yourself first, then others. Once you do this, no matter what the circumstances in your life, you'll know what works for you and it brings balance to your life as you lean into your vision. When tough times come, you'll be in a reliable flow that you know works for you. Add urgency to this energy by imagining it is your last day on Earth. This helps you feel what is important and what is not. Create decisions based on feeling. Do a breathing exercise and relax while marinating on your choices. If you repeatedly feel a warning signal when working with a certain person, i.e., feeling stifled, suffocated, or flat, you are being given signals of a loss of power. Walk away from anything that causes those feelings. Walk towards feelings of freedom and expression.

My wish for all of you is that you can experience the different ways Soul Mastery can be applied to your life and business, and I leave you with my recipe to follow.

The Recipe for Mindset Mastery

1. Once you are ready for mastery, you know it.
2. Once you arrive at this point, you never go back. The back door is closed.
3. You become conscious of your effect on the planet. You choose better products - for instance, non-plastic options - and once you are sacredly intertwined at the level of connection to Source, you make adult choices. They are solid, committed choices with a less negative impact on the planet, people, and animals.
4. You have more impact with influencing as you are freed up to speak authentically.
5. You take 100% responsibility for your actions, thus dropping the victim mentality even when bad things happen.
6. Your body and heart lead the way in decision-making. You are so in tune you feel the right direction within you.
7. Your boundaries become strong based on the attunement of your values. "No!" becomes a superpower as you step away from people pleasing or being liked in decision-making.
8. Your "Yes!" becomes instinctual. You freely say Yes even if you don't know how. Money, time, or not being good enough no longer stand in the way of your vision.

9. You handle your fear. It coexists with your wildest dreams, no longer forming your choices. Fear is seen as an impetus to moving forward, not stopping.
10. Reframing your experience of failure to a path not taken. There is no failure.
11. Deep understanding of cycles of life. Where are you on your path? Where do you choose to go? Allowing timing to open up to the right opportunities. Feeling into the opportunity and then using the body discernment to know if it's a yes or a no.
12. Taking action. No matter the circumstance. This is the Masculine.
13. Taking pauses and space. This is the Feminine.
14. You let go of perfectionism. Never going back to make something more perfect. Only moving forward in your expression. Creativity becomes a stream of consciousness until you die. So be in cycles of growth and death, not just the peak experiences.
15. Vulnerability attracts. Allow yourself to be seen as vulnerable.
16. You are willing to test yourself and be tested by the universe. That's the path you walk.
17. Be authentic. Be you.

In the following example, I show you how I influenced my client's visibility to align with authenticity.

Your Secrets are Your Access to Power:

Meet Natasha Nicole Harris, an Akashic Guide

From my perspective as her coach, I couldn't fully "hear" what Natasha was offering because she sounded vague when I first interacted with her. When we got deeper, I kept hearing her talk about Akashic Records, but always in the background. I asked her about this, and she said she didn't want to be seen as a "woo woo" type of person.

My sense with Natasha was that she did not allow herself to be genuinely authentic, as she feared being ridiculed. This is sadly true for so many entrepreneurs, because they think an aspect of their work could make them look stupid. Women have been at the forefront of this hyper-masculine way of being in that the spiritual realm has been discredited. Anything to do with hunches, gut feeling, instinct, divine guidance, divination, and healing has been said to be out of the realm of "successful business." The patriarchy has demonized the world of feeling and assigned it to women's whims. I urged her to bring this aspect of her work to the forefront of her brand and position herself as an Akashic guide.

The Akashic Records are deep within the realm of the Spiritual; "a compendium of all universal events, thoughts, words, emotions and intent ever to have occurred in the past, present, or future in terms of all entities and life forms, not just human…they are encoded in a non-physical plane of existence." Wikipedia

In some of her work, she leads profound meditations guiding her clients to the energetics of their deep calling. I had previously experienced the Akashic field when I was trained in meditation at a temple, where I pulled out a book and read about my previous lives, so for me, this was not "out there." Nevertheless, it's essential, deep-rooted wisdom and I took Natasha's work seriously. In the realm of the feminine, this is very much part of the mysteries and tapping into them gives us access to information that we wouldn't usually enjoy.

It's a vibration and a frequency. It's a flow.

I kept encouraging Natasha to be an Akashic guide as she was invisible to the clients who were an aligned fit for her. Finally, after two years, she took the time to express herself fully and is now taken very seriously by the business community.

Her work is no longer vague but precise, as shown in her bio:

Natasha is an Intuitive Business Mentor, Activator, and Healer. She guides 6-figure Soul-Led Entrepreneurs leaping to the next level of impact, success, wealth, leadership, love, and magic. Working with the Ancient Wisdom for the next level of energetic expansion activates a deep stirring in your soul to remember who you are. In addition, she offers Akashic Soul Readings.

Clarity is power.

Her client's experience of abundance isn't simply about money. Instead, the planet's happiness is more important than money to her. So how does abundance show up for her and her clients?

"For me, it's about Soul Wealth which isn't simply about money. Wealth is about that inner success, that inner alignment, the inner peace, the ability to navigate the challenges, the duality, and the polarity in life. Feeling wealthy in my life and relationships; it's how I communicate with people from a space of love and compassion, how I want to see the world shift and change and model that for myself. It's showing up in all areas of how I want to be me, in my relationships with my partner, my parents, my friends, my colleagues, with you, my coach, and leading myself with honor and respect and love—not beating myself up too much about getting it wrong or not showing up exactly in the right way.

It's no longer about right and wrong, it's about deepening and expanding everything. The visibility piece is never done as we consistently learn about who we are. So the visibility will always become more visible as we go through things, as we go through more challenges in life and business, and as we share our story, our passion, and what we hope for the world. The change that we wish for the world for humanity and nature and everything and I believe that as we show up more in our sense of honor in everything, we ripple that out. It's not just about abundance, it's about relationships, about who we are becoming and that leadership part of it then leads to the money as a result of that as we shift our belief in the area of money - we talked about it, the currency of love and inviting and receiving more of that in. So wealth for me is about everything else and then the money comes."

Find Natasha at https://mindbodysoulenergy.co.uk/

The following example is a client who altered traditional property development and invested it with spiritual mastery. This is the second thread of entrepreneurs I work with in conventional business, infusing it with New Earth spiritual mastery.

The Master Builder, Visionary Alex Impey of CoCity:

Alex's strong values came from childhood. Like many on the path of soul mastery, a few defining moments were the catalyst for him to become a visionary property developer. The conditions of a master are often created in response to difficulty, and for Alex, these were embedded into his experience. His father left his mother when Alex was three, and his mother brought him up as a single mother in a council estate in northern England. He didn't experience the council estate as a negative; instead, it ignited in him a passion early on for affordable social housing. His close connection to his mother, who loved watching sci-fi shows, led to a deep fascination with space travel. Having lost a father figure, he turned to the other men in his family to serve as role models and one of his uncles was a mechanical engineer who traveled extensively. These factors caused a stirring in Alex of his legacy vision.

After studying engineering at the University of Newcastle, he worked for Shell, becoming immersed in a corporate lifestyle with access to large sums of money. Unfortunately, money doesn't cause happiness. He had an inner crisis followed by an epiphany that caused him to turn toward a vision of a different kind of community that would serve people.

He bought a property with a partner in a development where the developer had segregated each block into different tenures: one block upmarket, one rental, and, as the remit for some councils is that all new developments have to include social housing, a block of council housing. The gentrification of a neighborhood can cause great stress for those living there. The council tenants disliked the posh neighbors; the upmarket homeowners didn't want the devaluing of their properties due to their proximity to council properties. Alex experienced a total breakdown in their relationships with neighbors. Isolated in each housing category, the neighbors were at odds with each other. It was then that his vision formed. If he could experience a great life in a council estate with a single mother and that life then supported him in getting an education and a promising career, how could it be that as a homeowner in a wealthy part of London, the community was in breakdown?

"There's got to be a better way," and the idea of flexible living was formulated. This is the call to the legacy of the one on the path to mastery.

So what is flexible living?

The community-centered, flexible living lifestyle is Alex's visionary plan. Put community, growth and flexibility together, creating a bespoke lifestyle based on "Live, Work, Play." This lifestyle allows people to live the best way they can and be the best version of themselves.

How does it work?

CoCity buys up existing buildings (recycling) and builds a mixed-tenure living experience (serving all ownership levels): some own, some rent, others have supported living situations, and everyone lives together. This vision is to help people from their early 20s through to their late 40s, thereby mixing age groups. There are also key ingredients to enhance connection, so incorporated into every site are restaurants, co-working environments, fitness studios, healthcare, and entertainment. It's a holistic view of the world. It's how people connect. Alex brought holistic spiritual life into his business.

When he came to work with me, his biggest issue was a lack of trust in anyone being able to do the job as well as he. A lone wolf, this caused friction in generating his vision. But, to grow big, we must trust others to delegate our ideas. As time has passed, working with levels of trust and using his innate powers of connection with people, he is focused on procuring suitable properties. He has found sustainable allies who fit out the interiors.

Delegating to partners in his world, joint ventures with financial groups who bring in the money to purchase properties, and building partners who want to showcase their specialist sustainable options means he works as the center of a wheel of energy, where others come to him. He can offer them opportunities for their work. One of the most powerful aspects of his work is that Alex doesn't hide his roots. He celebrates them authentically.

This hasn't been easy. He has had to muster all his other skills and values to commit to this New Earth community vision, including his ultimate dream of creating global communities with CoCity and then himself going to space (that's the Star Trek in the man). Never forgetting his ultimate passion, this year I guided him to go to tea with a billionaire property developer who has already gone to space. You have to align with your highest values as if they are non-negotiable, and while the journey on the ground is unfolding, take good care of your precious dreams. That's mastery.

You can find Alex's info here https://www.cocity.co.uk/

Here's to following your heart and your passion, allowing the unfolding, changing of the seasons, letting things die that no longer serve you, and nurturing your highest dreams. You are all masters of the mysteries.

"You are the master of your destiny. You can influence, direct and control your own environment. You can make your life what you want it to be."

~ Napoleon Hill

CHAPTER SIX

The Journey of the Heart and Mind

By Olga Brooks

23 years ago — half of my lifetime ago — I was standing on the street in the North End of the Italian quarter of Boston. This was the first time in many years I had been back here. I walked up and down Hanover Street to find the restaurant I used to work at when I first moved to Boston. Back then, my English was only good enough to say pleasantries to people and engage in small talk. I wasn't sure what was waiting for me in the future. My immigration status was at risk, and I was alone in this country — the country where so many people in the world wish to live.

When I returned to the restaurant I used to work, I ate my dinner with tears in my eyes, thinking of everything that had happened during the past 23 years. I stared at the door of the restaurant, where I could see my younger self, like a ghost, still standing there inviting people to dine, not knowing how my life would turn out. The young Russian girl who was able to make her way to the USA in the crazy '90s was now a distant memory. At the time, my mindset was open and flexible. I didn't have many fears because I was young, healthy, intelligent, and beautiful. Year after year, I was making it. My English improved fast, and soon I landed a job as a preschool teacher in a prestigious part of Boston where I worked for four years.

Everything seemed to be falling into place. I had a wonderful boyfriend. My immigration status was back on track. I was able to travel. I took art classes and acting classes. I had so many choices to live my freedom.

Everything seemed normal, like I was living my life just as I was supposed to, and just like everyone else. I'd made it. Until one day, the usual migraine headaches I suffered from came around and wouldn't go away for days. I couldn't get out of bed and go to work. Eventually, the migraine made my vision so weird and warped that it got to a point where I thought I was losing my mind.

At the hospital, my boyfriend came in with tears in his eyes, "You've had a stroke," he said. I had to look it up in a dictionary. I was only 27. Losing my peripheral vision and orientation scared me. I felt weak and lost. My dad kept telling me on the phone, "You are strong. You will make it through." I had to learn to walk again without falling from dizziness after losing my vision. It took time for my brain to catch up, so I kept bumping into things.

Inside buildings and on the streets my mind was confused, I had no idea where to go, which direction was correct. I didn't know whether I'd eventually reach where I needed to go or end up somewhere else entirely. I walked around like this for three years. I had to re-learn many things I used to know. But, despite my bad luck, I was alive. I leaned on the support and love from the people around me: those I worked with and the parents of the kids at school. And even though the recovery seemed so slow, I was able to go back to work a month later. My brain worked double time because I had to check with myself if I understood people correctly. I supposed I was going in the right direction, since I was allowed to stay on at work and was told I was doing better. But it was still so fresh and scary. Meanwhile, the doctors tried to figure out why someone so young had suffered a stroke. Surely, there was an underlying cause — was something else wrong with me. This started a constant fear for my health and my new reality shifted my mindset dramatically from the carefree 23-year-old who had moved to the US and "made it."

A year later, I got married and three years after that, my first son was born. Again, everything seemed to be falling into place, and

I was once more tagging along with how life should be — giving my body to other humans to grow and appear in this world. Taking care of a new soul kept me grateful for my health and abilities. I had found my new family in this foreign country.

While living a life that seemed so normal, deep down my heart was heavy and I felt like this life was not truly mine. How could I be living my dream life in America, with wonderful children, a beautiful home, and my freedom, but have a heart that was so deeply unhappy?

I was questioning who I was and my purpose in life. And I didn't have the answers. I was lost once again. The vision of my life was dark. The happiness of my heart would come only in spurts during precious moments of watching my children grow happily. But was that it? Is that how my life was always destined to end up? Some of my church friends were telling me it was normal. Everyone lives like this. Love fades and intimacy, too, after 17 years together. I couldn't accept that. How can that be? I came to this country with no English and managed to create a whole life for myself. Did I survive a stroke to live a life that felt so unfulfilled? Not only did my heart ache, but my soul was in a dark place.

The disconnect with my husband deepened my despair for living this life. My mind was stuck in a rut and I needed to adjust my mindset. Oh, I have learned how vital my brain is. If something, even the tiniest blood clot, gets into it, my body won't function. My vision and orientation never returned. And here I was again, disoriented, with no vision for tomorrow. Or that's what I thought. Another shift to my mindset was about to begin.

After many sessions with my therapist, I made my choice to divorce my husband and start a new life. But how do you start all over again when you are over 40? I was scared. I was frightened of my weakness. Afraid of my mind. What if I don't make it for my kids? The fear was debilitating. Even on that level, I understood that my strong abilities were not enough, and I had no tools to navigate my every day. I discovered that when fear is crippling, we are ruled by the mind and when we can overcome our fear, we have control over our mind. The latter is mindset mastery.

For the first time, I turned away from the chatter of my brain, and turned towards my heart. I discovered a new me. A me that could be happy. I stopped going to the therapist and to church and started exploring myself. I knew so much about the function of my brain, but I needed to learn about the mind. I was not opposing the church. This was the first step to understanding. But as my good friend Natasha told me, I had outgrown the church's walls. We all have God within us. And we all come from that source of knowledge. The source that we resonate with. And that source is the heart and mind. The universal heart that connects us all was another mindset shift that I came to embrace. But I had to learn all about that. And not only learn but put it into practice too.

At my lowest, I was mad at the Creator, asking him why he would give us this brain and then judge us for all its thinking. And I got my answer three years later: The mind is where our soul and spirit communicate. That changed it all for me. I got myself, through observation, into a state of clarity from the brain chatter. This awareness and ability changed my heart and my life. Being free from painful memories and living in the moment created more possibilities for a better future — a future where fear could be just a fleeting moment. And I am the one who chooses to be free of it. In that state, I became aware of the guidance within. There is nothing I need from the outside. We have our internal cellular connection to the divine. Remember all the prophets and saints. They got it. They mastered their minds to hear the higher guidance.

I felt I was right to be miserable in my relationship with my ex-husband. Because it felt that way. And my brain yet again confirmed it.

Until I read the book *Rewiring Your Soul* by Gabriella Kortsch, I started to understand that my thoughts are a byproduct of my feelings and emotions. And I have a choice of what to think and how to feel.

My fantastic discovery of the truth brought me to clarity and harmony. And now I am always focused on living in the present and choosing what is best for me.

I used to believe that all my thoughts were coming from my heart. I thought the emotions I felt were from my heart and my mind was a witness to it all. But when my mind became free of fear and judgmental thoughts, and memories of others and myself, my heart started sending me different emotions and messages. And that was liberating.

Looking back on the past, I was proud to be loyal to myself, honoring all my feelings and emotions because my brain confirmed everything.

I started making choices for my heart to feel freedom and love no matter my circumstances. I began to learn to be a witness to my thoughts, my heart's emotions, and my body. It started with the love in my heart — the love for the self on a level of the soul.

Looking in the mirror into my eyes, I saw the soul that was so deep and so real. And that soul was free. Free to live this life in love and abundance. The life of stability and success. I started to understand that fear is a made-up story. And that all began from the knowledge that I am the ruler of my mind. And that is where my strength and freedom are because the soul is free.

I see people are still struggling to align the heart and the mind saying, "My heart is at war with my brain." And I truly get that. This is the truth for so many people. Because without this unique understanding and the tools to navigate the mind, the heart will always be in battle. Unless we give in to the mind, the heart will always be in second place to guide us. The only way I found managing my life as a foreigner, a mother, and a woman doing things all by myself is by creating inner harmony, so balance seems like a byproduct of my inner peace. And yes, it became available to me only through a different mindset.

Days filled with responsibilities, obligations, and surprises are not always easy to manage and don't always help us stay sane. Those still chasing the balance will figure out when they are retired that this was simply impossible. But those who create harmony will enjoy their lives every day before they become old.

The fulfillment of the heart is the beauty of this life. Young minds know this like no one else. But then they grow up and become like most people. Tagging along with the demands of responsibilities and the way society is structured. We continually observe the heart's desires and their beauty from our TV screens, forgetting how to live them in our own lives. I pondered why that happens to most of us. And I found that our programmed mindset is conditioned to behave this way. But it doesn't have to be. I can be a hero to my children in my own life and teach them how to be one too. I have started teaching them about our minds and re-programming them to think differently.

Watching my marriage crumble and being faced with leaving the home I had made in this foreign country felt like I was losing my entire identity. The woman I grew into all those years ago. The wife I had learned to be. The mother of two boys whose parents will now forever have separate homes. Everything I had known was slipping through my fingers like sand, impossible to hold onto. Was the stroke the wake-up call that I had missed? I can't recall now. So much happened after that.

To master my mindset, and move forward healthily, I began to understand and practice living my soul's truth. I did this through knowledge and experience; we are spiritual beings first and only then are we physical.

I started connecting to my heart daily. I am faithful to my soul and my heart is open and happy. I notice the signs and small details around me that are guiding me towards the next step to take, and I see other people and respect where they are on their own journey.

Understanding myself helped me to stop judging others. And that is a state of mind that needs to be addressed and mastered. We all start by developing from our hearts in our mother's womb. And the soul comes into this world when we show up before our parents. So, we all start the same. But, during a lifetime, not everyone gets the same guidance and tools to navigate the journey. I am here looking back at myself at 23-years-old, a free and naïve girl who had no idea what lay ahead. And it is not because I am older and have the wisdom from my lived experiences. I wish I had known this information when I was young. Young enough to appreciate the beauty of this life and avoid heartache and depression. But here I am — the mother who has the chance to teach her kids the wisdom of the heart and mind.

When I started going deeper into understanding myself as a spiritual human, I learned how to move Universal energies through my body, getting rid of old memories that did not serve me. I learned how to stay healthy and protected from the influences of other people's negative ways of being.

Embracing the beginner's mindset, I started learning metaphysics and became certified in Sound Healing. Metaphysics opened a world of pure magic when looked at it with the human mind. Some things are magical, like Jesus's healing and turning water into wine, and helping people conceive a child using a few words. This field is a joy to explore because it brings hope to resolving many difficulties we often get stuck in over and over again. And that is why I also learned about our subconscious mind. We all have wounds. Our conscious mind doesn't remember why we have some fears and continuous anxiety or some physical ailments. But our subconscious knows it all. Working with the subconscious part of our mind brings total transformation and healing on a mental and physical level. My teachers have healed cancer through mastering their mindset and proper nutrition. This is not practiced on a broad level yet. But I believe this is the next step that many will take.

Our mind is amazing and so is our spiritual body. We only need the knowledge and the tools to make them work for the good of our souls and our lives on this planet. And that is why I am convinced that we should know this information when we are young. Then, so many illnesses can be avoided. So much harmony can flow into relationships, workplaces, and on to future generations.

It is nice to have your community at church. But what I have learned is that God doesn't do anything for us. He has already given us everything we need. So, connecting with the divine, not through neediness but through knowledge and unity, is a particular way of navigating this not-so-simple life.

This is the power of us spiritual humans. The loss and collapse in my life brought me new beginnings and allowed me to build a whole new home. It is in moments of hardship that we cannot foresee the future and the wisdom of our every experience in life. Looking back, we may recognize the blessings if we are awake enough and aware enough to see them. Now, I recognize that all my wisdom came from all my experiences: the bad, the good, and the ugly.

Reflecting on the time I had a stroke was a fantastic lesson for me. I am so much more connected to my body and my brain. But learning about the mind opened so much more.

The time before my heart surgery after the stroke gave me a glimpse into the realm behind the veil. We call it supernatural. But in reality, the everyday world exists around us and we all transition into it again after this lifetime. An astral projection experience at that time didn't wake me up fully to understanding. But my divorce and all the shuttering of my life did.

Mainstream education didn't bring the knowledge that life provided. And this education is free. If only we had more educated people in this area. I understand not every person going through rough periods ends up connecting to the universal knowledge of life and the mindset that transforms the future. But there is always an opportunity for it.

I have met so many people and made friends worldwide who took that chance to gain a more profound knowledge of us as spiritual human beings. Who had worked with their ego self that puts us in a scarcity mode. I had to address this and learn about my ego, which is a part of our awareness and the result of many outcomes of the situations we face. I know that today might be scary, but it all passes away because time doesn't wait, and things change with it. I learned to be aware of my ego, always looking out for me and trying to protect me. But with that comes fear and anxiety. Again and again, I would turn into my heart space, notice with my observer, and open it to freedom and love within. In that space, there is no place for fear.

I had mastered three things:

1. Transforming the fear of the ego mind
2. Spiritual awareness
3. Living by my heart

Conquering fear is the mastery of life, which means becoming the ruler of the mind. Of course, it takes time and practice. But an understanding of it is the beginning of the process. It is not only a mindset but a conversation with the fears. Becoming a loving parent to yourself.

We all hear about the importance of forgiving others because it's not for them but for you. I took my time with this one because I didn't have the tools. Yes, saying, "I forgive" helps but only for a short time because there is another component at play: memory. And when we remember what people have done to us, our emotions resurface. When we feel them again, it seems we didn't forgive after all because we didn't forget. I used a practice similar to Ho'oponopono. When I looked into the mirror and told myself, "I forgive you." Yes, the forgiveness of others starts with forgiveness of ourselves. This concept was taught in a loving, non-judgmental way. The peace in the heart begins with the forgiveness of ourselves. And it's liberating.

The feeling of being alone kept coming up every holiday or my birthday. This one I am still working on. It was not easy for me to find and hold strong friendships in a new culture, and during the period when I was going through divorce, it was especially tough. But over the past few years, I have become friends with amazing people like powerhouse celebrity Forbes Riley. I learned from the best, like Marisa Peer, who works with celebrities who are just like us and had their own childhood experiences, traumas, and transformations. Being amongst them to bring a difference into the world tells my 23-year-old me that I have made it.

If I never turned to the understanding of the mind, my heart would still ache. And my life would not be the same. So, my transformation started with knowledge and my decision to change what is into what I desire. And it all began with the journey of the heart and mind.

“You have power over your mind, not outside events. Realize this, and you will find strength.”

~ Marcus Aurelius

CHAPTER SEVEN

Embrace Your Light: Don't Let Your Light Be Dimmed by Your Past

By Haran Singham

"Our deepest fear is that we are powerful beyond measure.
It is our light, not our darkness that most frightens us.
We ask ourselves, who am I to be brilliant, gorgeous, talented, fabulous? Actually, who are you not to be?"
~ Marianne Williamson

In his hierarchy of needs, Maslow stated that every time you run away from your self–actualization, you're in conflict with yourself. First, you feel confused and frustrated with what you're doing with your life. Then, you become unfulfilled and unhappy.

Is the life you are living now creating a pathway toward self-actualization? Or is it taking you in another direction?

What is your purpose?

What is your passion?

What is your life mission?

Are you living the life that you want?

Do you have a mindset that believes that anything is possible?

You're saying no to life every time you say no to yourself. You're saying no to your loved ones and others you can impact. You are doing a disservice if you're playing it safe and staying in your comfort zone.

I'll be taking you through the journey I've gone through in my life—a journey from feeling unworthy, suicidal, and not good enough, to overcoming my trauma and changing my mindset into a true blessing.

It wasn't easy growing up in a war zone, experiencing family violence, war trauma, enduring sexual abuse, and not wanting to continue living the life I wanted. I remember a particularly traumatic event that occurred when I was about twelve years old. It was a rainy day and my family and I were hiding in a bunker with some other locals. Running away from home, we had tried to escape all the shelling and bombing. We knew we must be on the run often, so we always had a bag with first aid, dried food, and a couple changes of clothes. Our mindset was that of survival mode.

On this rainy day, we hadn't had a chance to have any meals. We were on the move, trying to save our lives and, in the process, becoming internally displaced. I was scared. My autistic sister was so terrified of the shells and bombs that she stayed inside the bunker, and I looked after her. Most of the children and women were inside this flooded bunker. Some men either sat or crawled on the ground. A few adults sat outside, telling everyone inside to stay hidden. We were worried that there might be some snakes looking for frogs in the bunker. I could hear some children and women screaming and crying. Most of us were terrified of the nonstop shelling that had been happening for a few days.

Subconsciously, I believed it was customary to live this way. This was the life I was exposed to and it was all I knew, growing up in Sri Lanka.

When it was safe, my family and I left that flooded bunker and returned to our house. I started going to school again. My parents had always prioritized my education above anything else. Usually,

I'd wake up at about 5 am, get ready, go to tuition class, and then go to school. After school, I'd attend tuition class and come home before 6 pm. If I didn't turn up on time, my father would interrogate me and often beat me up.

There was no electricity in the Jaffna district where I lived, because all the electric plants were destroyed by the bombing. Therefore, we had to use a kerosene lamp. There was an economic embargo, so most things were hard to buy in Jaffna. We couldn't watch television or engage in other time-passing activities that we take for granted in other parts of the world. We could use a bicycle dynamo to generate electricity to listen to the radio or play music.

While I was studying year 12 in Sri Lanka in 1996, the war reached its peak, forcing us to run away again. We moved to Colombo, Sri Lanka. My parents wanted me to finish high school in Colombo, but I was constantly getting arrested and taken away for interrogation by the Sri Lankan police or intelligence officers. Because of this, my parents never let me go anywhere alone. If I did want to go out, my parents either came too, or I didn't go anywhere at all. Even if we were staying in a motel, the police would conduct random checkups and would often take me away for interrogation. My mindset was set on my studies and my life revolved around school.

I was arrested yet again. The officer spoke to me in fluent Tamil, asking where I studied, where my parents were, and a few other questions. Then he asked me to sign the statement, which he'd written in the Sinhala language. I refused to sign the statement because I could not understand what was written there. When I asked him what was written on the report, he hit me a few times. Then he put one of his legs in between my legs and told me the next one was going to be "there," so "why don't you sign."

I didn't say anything; I signed the statement that he wrote. After that, my fingerprints and photos were taken and finally, the officers took me to the court. I had never gone to any court before in my life. I appeared in front of the magistrate for almost 30 seconds; however, I was not even asked a single question, and I had no lawyer. All the communication was done in Sinhala, so I had no idea what they were talking about. I was then placed in a cell with a few men who were there for other charges and hearings.

In court, my father had told me he would get me out of jail the next day; however, I was imprisoned for about a month. My father didn't tell me I would be in prison for that long. Every time he visited, I looked into his eyes and saw that he was hiding something. But I didn't want to force him to answer any of my questions. I was too tired and exhausted for anything, so I told myself that whatever happens will happen. I knew I had nothing in my control. It was a new experience for me. I wondered if I might lose my mind.

During my growing up years in the northern part of Sri Lanka, my parents were overprotective. I didn't even know how to buy something in a shop. Because my parents did everything for me, I focused only on my studies. For them to see me get arrested was very hard, and going through the nightmare of my imprisonment was even more challenging. I was just 17 years old then, and I was terrified. I felt as if I was in a deep jungle without any direction. The journey to the jail took about a few hours, and I felt like a criminal. I was unsure what was happening because I didn't speak any Sinhala, and could see my whole life disappearing. I have never felt so horrified, isolated, numb, and disoriented.

While I was in jail, I had to go through so much as well. I was put in prison with other criminals and endured sexual harassment from some prisoners and officers. It was a scary and disgusting time for me. I cried for many days, thinking that if I died, my parents wouldn't have to suffer. I felt as if I had brought shame to my family. Every time my father visited me in jail, I could see tears in his eyes. It was one of the darkest times in my life. This was the beginning of developing an unbreakable mindset. I realized I was much luckier than most. I had a fantastic family, supportive brothers, and money. However, an arrest can be terrifying for many, sending your mind out of control with worry especially those from poor backgrounds in Sri Lanka.

My father told me that the statement I had signed claimed that I was a Tamil Tiger (LTTE), smuggling arms and laundering money for LTTE. It was going to be very hard to get me out of jail. However, my father also told me that he'd bribed the judge and intelligence officers, who promised they would let me go home on my next hearing. I later discovered that my father had given Rs.100,000 (Rupees) to the intelligence officers and judge. That was a lot of money during that time.

Though I was released from jail at my next hearing, my situation was still dangerous. The police were still arresting and interrogating people, and I couldn't go anywhere alone while in Colombo.

On November 15, 1996, my father told me he wanted to take me out to buy some clothes. Once we were on the road, I learned I'd actually be flying to Melbourne, Australia. My father found an agent who organized the passports, boarding passes, and everything else for me to go to Australia. That night, I caught the flight and traveled with my passport, but I only had a visa to go to Singapore. Someone at the agency in Singapore gave me a boarding pass, and I arrived in Melbourne on November 16, 1996.

When I arrived in Australia, immigration officers took me to a detention center, leaving me alone. I thought I was in jail again and felt as if my life was in darkness. I couldn't see my future. I was terrified and unsure of what I could share with the officers, or if my life was in danger. I was back in the survival mindset and my thoughts began to betray me. *If they send me back to Sri Lanka*, I wondered, *what sort of details that I share with Australian immigration would be given to the Sri Lankan authorities?* Feeling incredibly scared and unsafe, I pulled the blanket over my body and crawled under it. A couple of days later, I was moved to a different area of the detention center with other asylum seekers. I was kept there for more than two and a half months. Finally, at the end of January 1997, I was granted permanent residency.

When I got out of the detention center, I stayed with one of my relatives for about a month. I had never met this relative before. However, I knew I was free. Since my English was very limited, I looked at completing some Engineering or Accounting diplomas so I wouldn't have to worry too much about writing essays or my English comprehension. Ultimately, I chose accounting because I was already familiar with accounting in Sri Lanka.

With a beginners mindset my first year after I arrived in Melbourne was wonderful. I did well with my studies. However, after my second year, I began cutting and burning myself. Depressed and very anxious about even small things, I started barely passing any of my subjects. I managed to get into university but was kicked out a couple of times because I failed most of my courses. I was in love with a girl from school, but it didn't work out, which further triggered my trauma. Once again, my mindset fell to pieces, and I wasn't confident I could put those pieces back together. As I longed for my family, dark days followed.

When I was in Sri Lanka, I had always considered myself to be an intelligent and bright student. Even though I wasn't outstanding in my studies, I prioritized them and did well. I was also a good sprinter and participated in competitions at district levels. However, after repeatedly failing a few subjects while at university, I started feeling stupid and not good enough. I couldn't figure out why it was hard to focus on my studies, why I was struggling with my memory, why I was having nightmares, why I didn't feel like I belonged anywhere, and why I was always sad. I just wanted to lock myself in my room and sleep. I didn't want to do anything with the world. I hated going out with friends or even hanging out with anyone. Even if other friends surrounded me, I always felt lonely and numb. It was easier to disappear and not get noticed. I didn't want to live in this world anymore. I just wanted to die. The only thing that accompanied me during this time was music.

When some of my university friends would ask me to go out, I'd say yes, and then I'd never show up. I felt that I wasn't good enough to hang out with them, and that they would see and reject the real me anyway.

During this time, I started connecting with the Sri Lankan Tamil community and singing Tamil songs on stage. When I was around people, I could put on a façade, but when I got home, my mindset was in a dark place. I was often self-harming.

I had no mental health awareness at that time. No words to express what was happening to me. I thought that was life.

When my current self meets my old self, I see a traumatized kid. One who went through so much trauma and never had the chance to process properly what he had gone through. He never knew that he could work on his trauma. He knew nothing about mental health, mindset, or mind management.

Most of the time I'd end up in my room, either sleeping or listening to music. My mood was up and down all the time. Sometimes, I'd go to a party or visit some friends, and feel so lonely—even though so many people were around me—that I'd have to leave the place. If I forced myself to stay, I would experience mood swings or get upset with my friends. So, most often, I would go back and stay in my room.

Some of my close friends suggested I speak to my doctor. I did this, and my doctor referred me to a psychiatrist and psychologist. So, I started seeing them, taking medication, and going to counseling for a few years. But nothing helped. I was walking around like a zombie and still feeling very depressed.

During this time, a friend introduced me to a Buddhist meditation teacher, so I started going to meditation classes. One day, while attending a class, I saw a flyer and business card for a life coach. I called, spoke to the coach about my situation, and decided to sign up with her for coaching.

Unfortunately, after eight weeks, I had to discontinue my coaching in order to go to the UK to visit my family. But while there, I realized I wasn't feeling depressed or moody. I thought I was happy because I was with my family. But even after returning to Melbourne, I felt great. I stopped feeling moody. I wanted to go out with my friends. I started to enjoy doing the things that others around my age would do.

My mindset had shifted in a big way and I started asking myself what the purpose of my life was. What did I want to do with my life, and why was I here in this world? I had been working as an assistant accountant for the Furnishing Industry Association of Australia. They paid me well and I knew that if I stayed there, I could continue growing in my career. However, I wasn't happy with what I was doing.

During this time, there were peace talks going on in Sri Lanka, and I decided to go there to volunteer at an orphanage and a shelter for people affected by the war. One of my friends from Sydney, Australia, also came to do volunteer work there. Even though she's Tamil, she couldn't speak Tamil properly, so I was her interpreter. Once, while walking on the street, we saw some school kids and started talking to them. My friend asked one of the little girls, "How old are you? What are you studying?"

The girl, who looked six years old, said, "I'm in year six."

My friend started crying because we could see how malnourished these kids were. I felt very guilty that I had wasted my time feeling sorry for myself and feeling depressed, rather than helping the people who'd been affected by the war. When I returned to bed that night, I decided I wanted to help.

I figured I could become a doctor, like some of my other friends, and come back to Sri Lanka to help these people. So, when I returned to Australia, I started looking at a few options to get into medicine. However, I realized it would be a long process to get into the field. I would also have to invest a lot of money to get a medical degree. Therefore, I decided not to pursue that route.

I then contemplated helping war-affected people by becoming a psychologist. But then I learned that psychology was a five-year degree, and I would have to specialize and complete further studies to become a qualified psychologist. That would take many years. So I also gave up on that idea, and instead studied Social Science (counseling) to get into the mainstream. I also started studying coaching, which helped me overcome my trauma and master my mindset for the greater good of humanity. I learned many different modalities and coaching methods from world-renowned coaches and spiritual teachers such as Dr. Tad James, Tony Robbins, Dr. Joe Dispenza, Dr. Deepak Chopra, Dr. Amen, Master Choa, Master Stephen Co, Sadhguru and many others.

Since then, I have been working as a counselor and coach.

While learning the methods and working with people, I had a spiritual experience that completely blew my mind. One day, I was sitting in an ashram and meditating. Suddenly, I saw everyone else around me look like me. I thought I was going crazy. I started analyzing my own thoughts and my experiences to understand what was going on, but couldn't understand what was happening to me. Whether it was another person, plant, animal, or mountain, I saw myself in everything. There was only "ONEness." I was in bliss and had tapped into a beautiful dimension I could not access.

I experienced that state for the first time. From that day onwards, I have often stepped in and out of that state.

After that experience, I decided to become a monk to serve more people and help them realize that they don't have to suffer in life. I went to India and stayed in many different ashrams. However, in our culture, if you want to become a monk, you must detach yourself from your family, friends, and other worldly desires. I wasn't ready to detach myself from my family or close friends. Therefore, I returned to Australia; however, I kept returning to India and learned many mindset tools from different spiritual gurus keeping my practice.

I then realized that I wanted to be with people and serve them, rather than meditating alone in an ashram or cave.

My life experiences had taught me to blame everyone and everything else in my life. I had given away my power, letting other people and external situations decide how I felt, lived, and behaved. I used to believe that when I was angry, it was because someone or some situation made me angry. When I was feeling sad, it was because someone made me sad. However, after I had the oneness experience, I realized I was projecting onto everything around me. I also learned how powerful it is to share these teachings with the world so there won't be any suffering.

When I was suicidal and unhappy, I knew I was blaming others. When I started working on myself, I started going within to see that I had the problem, and became focused on working on myself. However, after that oneness experience, I realized it's about "ONEness." We as ONE. All of us and everything is "I AM."

The world has conditioned our mind to look at everything and think that we are limited and powerless. It has taught us to focus on material success and the external world. Of course, there's nothing wrong with that; however, if that's your only focus, you can't complain about not feeling fulfilled with your life.

We thrive when we change our lives and take the journey from OTHERS to ME to I AM. "OTHERS" is the blaming state, where we believe others are the reason for our suffering. After we realize we need to work on ourselves, we do so to the extent that we focus only on ourselves—on "ME." But once we step into the space where there's no them or me and there's only us—"I AM"—we start thriving. We are not separate from anyone. We can talk about love, happiness, and fulfillment. Unless it becomes your experience that we are ONE, you'll discriminate against others, judge others, and complain about life. Life becomes YOU versus OTHERS.

Some people experience trauma, or have gone through some horrible life experience, and don't work on healing. They try to create a happy and fulfilled life and fail miserably. If you don't heal your past, it will always come back and haunt you. You can only see the world through those lenses. Therefore, you must work on your trauma if you want love, happiness, or fulfillment in your life.

There's too much emphasis on the past in counseling. When I saw my psychologist, I was only talking about my problems and the past, and every time I walked away from the session, I felt miserable. We need a holistic approach to helping people heal.

After becoming a coach, one of the hardest things I did early on was working with an asylum seeker who had been gang raped and tortured by the Sri Lankan armies. As a form of protection, this person's brain had blocked out the trauma he had gone through. For a long time, he had no recollection of the event. But he had nightmares almost every day, and couldn't live a day-to-day life. Mentally and emotionally, he struggled so much. After we worked together, he began sleeping better, stopped having nightmares, and started living a life of his choice. After going through the coaching, he started smiling more and living a happier and healthier life. He invited me to his wedding a few years later.

For many years, another client of mine named Kate had been physically, emotionally, and sexually abused by her ex-husband. After she divorced him, she became suicidal. She stopped believing in herself, cried almost every day, and couldn't focus on anything else. She only lived because of her son, and thought she could continue without reconciling what had happened. However, she became so angry and reactive toward her parents and son, and hated herself for it. After we worked with her past trauma, she became a happier person and is now getting her master's degree in nursing. She now has an unlimited mindset more focused on the present moment.

Unless we reconcile our past and heal, we can't move on and create the life we want. There are tools and techniques available to help you overcome your past trauma. Some of these techniques allow you to work on it and heal, so you can move on with your life. You don't have to sit down on a therapist's couch for years, repeatedly talking about your past.

Only when you heal and learn to love yourself truly can you love others. That's when you can step into the I AM and ONEness reality mindset. Otherwise, your unconscious mind will project your past on everyone around you.

This is my mission: helping people experience that "ONEness" mindset and thrive in that "I AM" reality. Being in ONEness keeps this whole universe in balance. Because everything is one, you'll realize that you are not separate from the world around you. ONEness connects you to this universal intelligence. It's not a logical process you can sit down and go through. However, to help you understand this logically, I'd like you to feel the boundary of your body. As you do this, expand your body's limits into a sphere of awareness that surrounds your body. Now, imagine this field getting larger and larger, enveloping all the objects around you. This book you're reading becomes one with you, the world around you become one with you, and you keep expanding the sphere of awareness until everything becomes one with you. This gives you an overwhelming sense of peace. You become one with everything. There is no separation between you and what is around you. There's only "I AM" awareness.

When you're with other people, get into this sphere of awareness and include them as part of you. You will become empathetic. Your communication and understanding will become a lot more effective, especially if you are in any significant relationship. For example, imagine you're in business and are doing a sales call or talking to your boss. You become one with this person. When this happens, you understand them on a much deeper level. Imagine what would happen to your business and relationships if you lived in this state.

We change our lives and impact the world not because of what we do but because of who we become. This sums up the journey I've taken to transform my mindset, and how I help others change their lives. When I was going through trauma and struggling so much, I was still holding onto my past. I was holding onto my old identity and personality. Every change in the external world comes from the inner world. Nothing else will change around us when our inner world doesn't change.

Without shifting our identity, we cannot change our current reality. Most people focus on action-taking and having the best strategy. Yes, we must take action. However, we cannot change what's happening outside without internal shift. Otherwise, we will only self-sabotage our growth. When we look at all these multimillionaires and billionaires, we see them taking massive action. We think we need to take action too, so we focus on doing so. However, we don't know how much inner self-work these multimillionaires and billionaires have done. We don't have a strategy problem; we have a mindset problem.

I have a friend who has been trying to start his business for over two years. Every time I'd talk to him, he'd tell me how he's been planning and what actions he would take. However, all he was doing was self-sabotaging and never really getting started. After our initial conversations, I realized he had self-worth issues and didn't believe that he could succeed in his business.

At the end of the day, you can have the best action plans and strategies, but if your inner world is chaotic, you won't achieve what you want. You won't be able to create the life that you want. Therefore, I strongly believe in having a strategy, but that alone will not help you if you don't believe in yourself.

You'll see many introverted people, such as Bill Gates or Elon Musk, who have changed at different points in their lives. Their identity, worldview, and convictions have changed because of what's needed from them at a certain level. I've found this to be true for me as well. In the past, I was a tranquil and reserved person. Then, I discovered how I wanted to impact the world and live my life purpose. I realized I needed discipline to be this certain personality that my life purpose required. I embarked on that discipline journey and therefore, I ultimately created a different identity that is true and authentic.

I continue to evolve at different points in my life. We all do. However, are you consciously stepping into an identity that's going to serve you? If you had spoken to me about 20 years ago and told me that I'd be choosing a career that involves coaching people, talking in front of hundreds and thousands of people, or even writing a book, I would've laughed at you and called you crazy. Now I am doing all that and more because I shifted my mindset around my identity and my inner world.

When I got into coaching and counseling, I told myself that if I could even transform one person's life, I would be happy. Now, instead of one person, I've impacted thousands of people's lives within the last fifteen years.

When I impact other people's lives, I know I am living my purpose. So my life mission is to help people self-realize, and understand that suffering is optional. It's to help those affected by the war in Sri Lanka, and to give back to the Australian community by assisting the Australian Aboriginals. Ultimately, it's to guide people to be aligned with their higher selves and live their true purpose.

Whenever I work with someone and positively impact their life, I feel blessed, humbled, and energized. My life experiences and the trauma that I went through, were harrowing. What I've gone through has not been easy, but without those life experiences, I wouldn't be where I am today. So, the life that I am living now is a blessing. I believe my life is happening for me and that comes through an expanded mindset.

I help many individuals transform their pain into power, coaching people one-on-one and in groups. This journey has also led me to coach managers, CEOs, and directors, helping them build a healthy work culture, foster a productive team, and adopt better leadership skills by developing their emotional intelligence through a oneness mindset.

What I've gone through in life has helped me realize that I don't want to waste any of my time doing anything that I feel is meaningless. I know that I am here for a purpose: to serve. Therefore, I choose to live that purpose. This is where I find that meaning and fulfillment in life.

Our life is so precious, don't waste it.

“Change your thoughts and you change your world.”

~ Norman Vincent Peale

CHAPTER EIGHT

When Life Winks at You Opening to the Synchronicities

By Eve Kundycki

I was 33, in hot and humid Asia, wishing to understand life. With my hand on the black wooden commode, I stared at myself in the mirror. I took a deep breath and closed my eyes, feeling shame, despair, and the desire to be free from this confusion. Why am I here? How does this all work? Why does it feel like it's never good enough? Finally, after decades of life glitches but also beauty and joy, I wanted to better understand the human condition.

Aren't I supposed to be an "adult" by now? Something felt wrong with the way I functioned. Even with hopes and dreams, I seemed to bump against walls I could not comprehend. My desire to have a child was tangible. My heart silently expressed: "Please, let me heal before having my own children…" I didn't want to pass this confusion on.

I felt lost within myself; like it was me against the world. My mindset was a mess and without focus.

It wasn't a beautiful sunset, but the moment is engraved in my mind like a polaroid: a mundane picture representing a powerful inner prayer.

Have you ever had a moment when you felt your soul set an intention so deep?

Three years later, I was 36 and lying down on cold tiles, having contractions for hours. Even though the fetus was so tiny to release, the contractions felt excruciating. I surrendered to being so present with it, accepting that I had to endure the pain because of my decision to terminate the pregnancy. I had always wanted to be a mother, yet I had swallowed medication that would release from my womb that which awakened my biggest fears. I understood little about how expansive the journey that I had entered was.

Things sometimes get worse before they get better. I still believed it was me against the world. Even my own body felt like it was against me.

Two years later, I was 38 and traveling with a man I had met a few months earlier. I felt raw. Both of us were licking wounds from our past relationships. While examining my previous breakups, I was rudely awakened, clearly seeing my responsibility in them for the first time. My eyes had been opened to my codependent tendencies. I had uncovered the damage my childhood wounds and defense mechanisms had wrought throughout my life, pushing away those I loved most. I was rebuilding after heartbreak and an abortion.

Liam showed up as a patient witness to my recovery. Our trip together turned out to be a nurturing, healing pilgrimage. So often around my birthday, weird stuff happens; pivotal moments, as if the body and the nervous system know a different, transformational calendar. I treated myself to a dive in Roatan. I let myself fall backward, full dive gear on, at a spot called Mary's Place.

During this time, I was doing practices for *A Course in Miracles*. I could feel my teacher smiling at a symbol of Christ's Consciousness enveloping me. My mind surrendering to the unknown waters, I was in awe of the glistening underwater fireworks of fish and coral. As I moved weightlessly through the water, I was delighted to suddenly see a flamboyant nudibranch.

Nudibranchs are one of the stars of the diving world. These underwater clowns can be hard to find. It was beautiful to realize that, for many, the highlight of diving wasn't seeing the biggest fish, the greatest pleasure came from observing the rarest and hard-to-spot creatures; the quiet, subtle beauties. Once you start noticing these mollusks, more become visible. Like good dancing, good observation requires balance and a certain level of detachment to keep the mind open to what shows up. I feel similarly about synchronicities, which made me think of the role they had begun to play in my life.

* * *

The term 'synchronicity' was coined in the 1950s by Swiss psychiatrist Carl Gustav Jung to describe uncanny coincidences that seem meaningful. The Greek roots are syn-, "together," and Khronos, "time." We all occupy the same space. Jung, who founded analytical psychology, believed that human beings are connected to their ancestors through a shared set of experiences called the collective unconscious.

Synchronicities are experiences that seem far too meaningful to be mere day-to-day chance encounters. These 'winks from God' appear significantly related but have no discernable causal connection. The logical mind cannot explain it, yet there is an undeniable sense of link.

Have you ever had a moment of wonder and surprise when you bump into someone you were just thinking about? Have you experienced playful or more intense forms of wondering "what are the odds of this happening now?"

My mindset profoundly changed once I became more aware of synchronicities in life. I began experiencing the underlying magic of everything. This mindset shift didn't come from reading about it in books but from living it in the flesh. When the 'winks' started to appear more frequently, I softened. I developed a sense of being connected to something grander than all of us, something that connects all of us.

Synchronicities spoke in a different way to my senses. An understanding arose with more heart and less head, with more intuition and less logic. I was invited to change my mindset to be open to what I didn't understand. My attitude shifted to listening more to love's whispers of what life wanted to share rather than drowning them out with my personality's thoughts and opinions. I no longer forced what I wanted out of life but instead stayed open to the experiences life was inviting me into.

Gradually — from an embodied perspective — I began to understand that my soul was having a human experience with this body as a temporary suit but that it also possessed a clarity born of the experience of humans throughout the ages, a multiple-lifetime experience.

I only wondered, "How can I keep my heart open to everything that shows up?"

* * *

Meanwhile, back in Roatan, I finished my dive and was climbing out of the water when I saw the name of the boat, 'Diva'. It shared the same name as my beloved black cat who had disappeared during my recent heartbreak. When I felt Diva's energy, it was as if a guardian angel was watching over me.

A man onboard introduced himself. The universe was jokingly winking again. He had the same name as my ex-partner, the father of my baby who had never been born. I felt nauseous, unsure if it was from the waves stirring my stomach, my unprocessed emotions, or both. I tried to let go of attempting to construct any meaning from the event and take some deep breaths while feeling the discomfort. I intuitively saw my system was showing me where more healing was necessary.

Cosmic humor continued to surprise me at one of our next stops. I felt a calling to see Tikal, a Mayan citadel in the rainforest of

Northern Guatemala. We had to stay overnight in the village across the border in Belize. While driving there, we passed a sign with the town's name written in giant rainbow-colored letters. "San Ignacio." The air thickened in my lungs. My attention sharpened with a slight fear. The name in front of my eyes was also the name of my unborn baby. Even though I hadn't been able to 'receive' him, I had wanted to honor his soul in a ceremony guided by a priest. The giving of a name had been recommended. Looking into a burning candle, the name 'Ignatius' had come to me with clarity bowing me over. I'd never heard the name before. Seeing it here again was a sign, far more profound than a coincidence. I knew that I was answering a whispered call from my soul to visit Tikal, but I had no idea the visit would hit so close to home.

Arriving at our destination, I witnessed the location and suddenly saw myself. A part of my energy seemed to be outside of my body. I felt the heat in my feet and the blur in my brain. What was this? Did I fear that something was being called to my attention? Was I meant to do something? At my core, there was a reassuring quietness telling me to relax. I got out of the car and stepped towards the hotel. It was warm outside but I had goosebumps on my arms, my throat was tight, and I felt a wavering sensation. I turned to the side, looking for my luggage. I was surprised by a massive mural of a fetus a few stories high on the facade across the street.

We went upstairs, found our room, and dropped off our suitcases. In the kitchen was an ample window framing this giant yet-to-be-born baby.

I surrendered with a sigh. I recognized I had more to process regarding the abortion. I prepared myself for the wave of emotions that might arise. I was confused and curious. Would something more specific be conveyed to me?

After an early rise and some bouncing around on a bumpy road, we approached the ancient site. I was grateful to Liam for bringing me here; I love it when a man organizes logistics! I felt seen but also a bit nervous.

We approached the grounds through high trees. Accompanied by a woody, resinous smell, I heard and saw a group of locals participating in a dance ceremony. Tourists were taking pictures, but my attention was pulled elsewhere.

I felt a strong resonance with the location. A vibration rose inside of me. Then, stunned, I had inexplicable flashes: visions of having been here before, of human sacrifices, of a child offered to the gods. But it was more than visions; it was a simple knowing.

There was a strange sense of understanding and peace. Like a connect-the-dots, a bigger picture divulges. I saw my baby's father as a conquistador. I saw a love story cut short by sacrifice—the contradicting honor and despair of losing the fruit of the womb in the name of devotion.

A cold shower feeling washed over me, resulting in a warm, peaceful glow that traveled through my veins. A different understanding of life again. An experience so true and baffling.

The Mayan citadel towered over the jungle. From the top, I sat and contemplated this past-life experience feeling. Had I played a role that had been repeated many times throughout millennia? Was my experience a replay of the Tikal events in modern clothing?

Deep inner stillness infiltrated me—a strange peace inside the pain. I understood why some energies were so overwhelming. I felt the immensity of this network that connects us all through time and space while gazing from a seemingly full-circle bird's eye perspective. I had a sense of closure. Only awareness was here and a softening of the heart; no one was left to hurt.

I could feel the underlying energy of life that is ever-present, a tapestry into which is woven all that has been and will be. Life's bruises were soothed by its poetry, art, and humor.

There needed to be no fighting. It wasn't me against the world, but me as part of the world, open to what life wanted to show me.

Synchronicities brought me a lot of healing this way.

* * *

This story was borne out of an experience of lost love and abortion, a process that is often greatly misunderstood and a significant trial for anyone — especially for any woman who goes through it. The decision to terminate should not need to be justified. Now, as I guide individuals and couples into healing, and mindset expansion. I see that abortion more common than I thought, and the imprints it can leave are impactful. As charged a topic as it can be, I could not reflect on the full complexity of the termination in this chapter. Every experience is different. Lifting the shame and taboo can bring more understanding. In this context, there is perhaps value in sharing a glimpse of my own experience to assist you to master your mindset with the flood of emotions that are inevitable after an abortion.

I was 36, and even though I had always wanted to be a mother, something powerful in me knew it wasn't the right time. I deeply loved the father, but we didn't know how to function with each other constructively. Our chemistry was electric, bringing out the best and worst in each other. I didn't know then what I know now about conscious relationships and how they show us where to grow. We had already separated by the time I discovered the pregnancy. We used protection. The dates didn't add up. It happened right after a course at Mystery School, and just as mysteriously, I'd had my period the first month. It didn't make sense.

My situation felt overwhelmingly complex at the time: not having a fixed home, transitioning jobs, and being burnt out after a previous separation from a 13-year relationship. I felt unsafe and I was in survival mode, triggered into deep wounding. I distrusted existence and men, and I doubted myself.

Esther Perel, a relationship expert and Belgian like me, writes that only two relationships resemble each other. The one you have with your parents or the people that raised you, and the one with the people you fall in love with. It is often annoyingly 'textbook.'

My imprints were so profound. I only saw my childhood projected onto my future: an absent father, not being provided for, and the difficulties of being a woman and single mother in our society. I was overwhelmed. I didn't see another way out of what I thought was love for this baby and myself. And there was the fear of bringing into the world a being I would love so much and possibly lose.

* * *

The reticular activating system is a filter between your conscious mind and the unconscious mind. Our system adopts filters to prevent overwhelm by the daily exposure to trillions of data. This apparatus spots plenty of red cars if you are interested in red cars. It also keeps us blind to what we don't believe. Like colored glasses, based on our conditioning, the beliefs programmed in our early childhood, our culture, our environment, and what helped us survive, our system filters based on what we have learned and adopted to be true. The information may be present, the eye may see it, and the ear may hear it, but it may not be revealed to our senses as it is considered irrelevant.

At the time of the termination, my colored glasses were blind to solutions.

I wish every woman felt supported and safe to share when the most difficult decisions (at least it was for me) must be made. And I want safety and support for the men involved too. Every experience is different. I had no idea the multiple ways it would affect me later. I feel I would have chosen differently based on what I know now. But back then, it felt like the best and the only solution.

At that time, I was in “labor”; I gave birth to another me, a humbled version of myself with much more understanding for others and the human condition, with less judgment. As contradictory as it may sound, the termination was my wake-up call to more compassion and gentleness with myself. To heal, I needed to reparent myself with so much gentleness.

In retrospect, this period of my life was a very uncomfortable, intensive form of training to hold a loving presence for myself first. It became a pivotal moment, a reality check on my functioning. The healing I went through initiated a deeper, more powerful space and transmission for the recovery of others. My experience anchored an understanding of more than what meets the eye. Instead of judgment, I had to invite deep acceptance and grace. This resulted in me being more available to be in service to others.

The boundary between myself and others had begun to dissolve, and that process continues today. As a result, I feel less alone in the world and more inseparable from the world, constantly connected to it.

* * *

I sit here many years after my time spent in Guatemala and while the story of what happened there is complete, the magical healing power of the synchronicities continues. Pandora’s box had opened. I smile at how experiences, like different verses in a song, play on repeat at different levels. On a personal level, on an interpersonal level, and finally, in service of the collective.

Recently, I moved house and needed some things that had been in storage for years. Drafting this chapter coincided with reopening boxes containing clothes and other personal items related to the times mentioned above. I felt detached; I could let go of some things, and that letting go released sneaky lingering aches. I saw a divine timing, an order in things.

I was reminded that on the day I discovered I was pregnant, I met a man called "Unborn." Cosmic humor. I had never met anyone with that name and have never heard the name again since. I stay open to the idea that it might have always been planned like that.

A week after the end of my pregnancy, my computer crashed. Nervous about the verdict of what was wrong at the Apple counter, the technician confirmed: "Your Motherboard is damaged." No kidding. The laptop I bought to replace it actually "died" during what I'm writing here—again, closing a chapter.

I decided to meditate and do a ritual in preparation for writing. I received flashes before my eyes of human sacrifices, heads rolling down. That powerful image ruffled my feathers. Minutes later, on the other side of my window, I was surprised by banging noises. For the first time, without my permission, someone had climbed the coconut tree in my garden, slashing the coconuts that fell to the ground, one after another, like the heads rolling I had just seen in my vision. Someone in the village had passed, and they needed coconuts for offerings.

I had been sure that John Spender, the creator of *A Journey of Riches* who invited me to write this piece, knew Liam. John assured me they had never met before. I believed him, of course. Later, John messaged me.

"Guess who I'm meeting with?"

"Liam?"

It couldn't be, but it was. I didn't know they were in the same part of the world. Liam's path and mine took different directions a while back. We are on good terms but not often in contact. It's funny they met when I had just been writing about him. John followed some of our pilgrimage footsteps and was introduced to connections there.

A psychic did a reading for me and, without knowing anything about this story, brought up that my womb was grateful to me. That after multiple lifetimes, another way of feeling connected to life and God was present that didn't require sacrifice.

* * *

So, what is the use of synchronicities? What do they mean?

I can share what they meant to me. And I invite you to experiment for yourself.

When I notice synchronicities arise, it's like a confirmation I'm on the right path, that I'm in sync with the universe. Communication is happening between the inner world and the outer world. I feel an intimacy with life, life as an accomplice, a partner. Yes, sometimes it shows up with sarcastic humor, but it makes a dear humorous friend.

I listen to the messages and see the bridge between my consciousness and the unconscious. I see my connection to others. I read in the outer reflections, glimpses of what is happening below the surface in me.

It has been a journey into truth. My head had dismissed many messages of life because it didn't make "sense" according to the norms I grew up in to pay attention to those signs. Synchronicities invited me into feeling with an open heart, into connecting deeper with my intuition. They revealed the relationship to a grander scheme, connections between the objective and the subjective world, where life knows better than I do why something is meant to happen, and I can let go of my judgment. I released a certain self-centeredness and opened more to consider the divine.

Synchronicities have been magical, "tough love" guides for learning and doorways to enter. To be open to them opens my heart more fully. With this heart, I can share with others and judge less. It has been very healing.

I realized I denied a part of my reality, invalidating an available, present, and alive perspective around me. Since opening that renewed relationship with life, I have rarely felt lonely.

* * *

While my story highlights my process, everyone's experience will be different. I've found that in moments of clearer communication between realms, it feels like life slows down. It is subtle yet tangible. An awareness is present that something meaningful is happening. Those are the moments to listen.

Please, don't take my word for it. I invite you to explore for yourself. We each have a unique curriculum, so be open to seeing how synchronicities appear for you. Observe the energy, what is meaningful and speaks to your world of symbols, as it speaks to your senses and emotions.

It may be helpful to know some common ways synchronicities can appear.

Repetitions and symbols:

When things come in threes or multiples, it's often a vital sign of a message. They come in multiple ways, from universal, cultural, or personal symbols. They are meaningful confirmations, especially when coming from different sources. A classic example is seeing 11:11, but that is just the tip of the iceberg. Repeating numbers, words, names, animals, logos, dates, or even a color or detail that pops out to call for your attention.

These repetitions have a different flavor than a simple coincidence. Details connect in ways that resonate with you. For example, I notice signs sometimes appear as if you're wearing 3D glasses.

External events that mirror an internal process:

The same topic of conversation you've had internally shows up initiated by someone else externally. Book titles, headlines, lyrics, and even Instagram posts appear in unrelated circumstances and with different people. Okay, sometimes Google has a hand in that, so when you've researched travel to Bhutan, and your feed has all sorts of Bhutanese things, it might be less synchronistic. But if your hairdresser displays a book on Bhutan, it is a great time to book a ticket.

Notice how themes that awaken your curiosity are also discussed around you without you initiating them. Again, often in a series of events coming from different sources. Life has this way of giving us clues. It can happen in dreams, journaling, movies, and daily life. Nature reflects and communicates with a wind burst, a sunbeam, a bird's song, a door slamming, and events that seem to confirm an experience or call for attention.

Perfect timing and opportunities:

When a series of supportive events are carried out easily, like being at the right place at the right time, or a person pops up in your awareness then you bump into them soon after. Getting the unexpected opportune phone call, finding the missing tool, discovering a puzzle piece, having an idea, and then having the perfect opportunity arise.

On the other hand, sometimes synchronicities show that something is not meant for you. This can manifest when repetitive resistance, cancelations, and such invite you to change course. There is no need to force it. However, checking what is needed to make it flow is good, as it can be an invitation to redirect. Sometimes there might be a coinciding ending, departure, or closure. See the continuity of the message.

Connections:

Smells, sounds, or music that suddenly awaken connections with clarity. Your senses and emotions are engaged. A song that plays in the supermarket, a stranger's perfume, a name mentioned in a random conversation, or an image in a magazine. It can be a combination of the above, where links appear springing from different sources.

Sometimes, with the desire to make connections and find synchronicities, we start orchestrating them. This exaggerated manufacturing of connections is called 'apophenia.' However, when we actively look for evidence of something, chances are we will find it. So how do we trust that we are not artificially manufacturing them?

It's different when links occur unsolicited and are so real they can't be denied. Synchronicities have this way of awakening awe.

First, taking action in the direction we are called is excellent when in flow. It's different to grasping. Much depends on the intention and how relaxed the body feels at the time.

These are tips on how to experience synchronicities in a more grounded way.

Being the observer with openness:

Leaning into the witness's perspective with an open heart. It is recommended to set the intention to connect with synchronicities without force: "I am open to seeing what life wants to share."

I've noticed the importance of receiving information with spacious curiosity and free from judgment.

I am not questioning what comes, I am staying neutral with it, and receiving the information without grasping it or pushing it away. No craving, no aversion.

This doesn't mean it is void of emotions; quite the contrary. The feelings are there to be witnessed too.

Being self-aware of the feelings and emotions from a neutral space, without letting yourself be carried into the story or judging them, is a gift. Like reading a book, you don't have to make up the story; you keep following and reading as it unfolds. Not being attached to the correctness of the story, not identifying with it, or trying to contain it. Don't let your mind attempt to fill in the blanks; let life expand.

Sitting with the trigger:

Whether in public life, relationships, or witnessing synchronicities, I have noticed the power of staying present even when some trigger takes the nervous system on a reactive ride. This doesn't mean suppressing or denying. Instead, it means feeling what moves through, with deep awareness, in continuation of being the observer. I call it "sitting with the trigger." This softening is a healing superpower.

It is easier said than done, but many things unveil in those moments.

In relaxing, breathing, and surrendering to a situation's discomfort, powerful healing happens.

Trust:

Allowing space to believe in the invisible. What doesn't feel welcome at your door might not show up. Experiencing synchronicities is a gift of life, like the universe whispering in your ear. It is like art; humbling to see the greatness of life and its creative force.

If a messenger is permanently questioned or ignored, he might stop communicating or come and bang on the door louder and louder.

It's like a balancing dance, in which being grounded and light on the feet helps. It is a beautiful dance of presence.

* * *

But are synchronicities always good? That's part of what synchronicities taught me: good and bad are relative.

Synchronicities can guide us to remarkable moments and to what appears as near-insurmountable challenges. The universe is concerned with our expansion, not our comfort. In the long run, our suffering hopefully leads us to our most significant growth. However, it is often only in retrospect that the value of our most difficult and painful experiences becomes apparent.

Signs have invited me into chapters of life that I couldn't have imagined. I am deeply humbled by and grateful for them, as they have forced me into becoming who I am today with a much more loving and spacious heart. This has been my invitation to self-actualization.

Life has a curriculum aligned with us in different ways—a unique personalized path.

When we look at another person as a human just like us, with insecurities, fear of the unknown, loneliness, quirks, and half-acknowledged feelings of helplessness, when we expand to feeling this, the heart opens towards the person with love. My journey has taught me that humans desire to belong, to be loved, to be accepted, and appreciated; to be truly seen. It's good to remember we are one human being to another. Also, that together, we are one being. Perfectly imperfect.

I used to feel like it was me against the world. Now after a powerful shift in my mindset I feel beautifully held by life and loved as part of it.

There is poetry to life, something mystical and mysterious that works through us often beyond our comprehension. Sometimes we are here to play roles for each other's curriculum of self-realization.

Personality-wise, stories seem juicier with a hero and a villain. But in the grand scheme, there are no labels, just life. Just love.

When I've loved life, I was open to seeing how much life has always loved me back. This is a form of mastery that broadens our sense of self and our surroundings.

May synchronicities show you that you are deeply connected to life's web. May you see the evidence of how life supports you in becoming the most authentic version of yourself.

May these winks from the Source bring you to your highest self and support you in all your relationships.

"All the world's a stage,
And all the men and women merely Players;
They have their exits and their entrances,
And one man in his time plays many parts."
~ William Shakespeare

"You need to overcome your fear-based mindset to live as your true self."

~ T. Harv Eker

CHAPTER NINE

Your Mind can Transform Your Life

By Andrea Gabriel

I would say my husband's negative mindset led to our marriage's demise.

We all have access to positive, negative and neutral mindsets. The mindset that most dominates our thoughts dictates how we experience our life. Often we become trapped in a negative way of thinking because we have discovered that being a victim actually gets us attention. After all, when you are a small child, possibly unheard by parents, any attention is better than no attention.

We all have a story, and for the most part, that story involves some hardship, whether it be abuse, abandonment, or neglect. And during these traumatic, vulnerable and deeply saddening times, we formulate characteristic traits that become our identity. Our personality will most likely take on obvious changes as we move through lifecycle periods. These changes often result from survival techniques we deem necessary to cope with life at one time or another.

Severe trauma can be suppressed deep within the nervous system, to a point where we can forget the severity of the trauma – especially if we were young when we experienced it. Hence, we can function in what seems like a normal life. However, when we don't have the means to release the impact of trauma, we develop dysfunctional behavioral or habitual patterns that become our coping mechanisms. Our inner child never leaves us. We grow, are (for the most part) institutionally educated, age and, in appearance, become adults. Sometimes these adults retain destructive personality traits. If we are unable to speak our truth and become submissive in life, we may take on aggressive, controlling survival patterns and obsessive-compulsive mannerisms; if we understand the truth of who we are, we may become depressed.

When we are not coping well with life and aren't sure why, it's common to self-medicate with recreational drugs, alcohol, cigarettes, food, sugar, or pharmaceutical medications.

The two ways I approached this challenge. I practiced self-loathing and chose addictive behavioral patterns for the earlier part of my life; then once I found a way to gain mental clarity and an awareness of the vibrational impact of energy and mindset within my life, I was able to embrace self-love.

Love is a gift that we receive from the universe. The purest vibration creates a strong feeling of connection and the ability to identify with all things. It's through love that we learn to master our mindset. It creates unity, which in its essence, shifts our perception from "me" to "us." Love has an uplifting and empowering effect when we experience it. True love is different from passion, which is short-lived and often comes from attraction alone. However, passion can evolve into true love if we choose to love unconditionally.

Love is soft and slow; love creates space to grow. Love gives to self first through gentle thoughts and actions. Love begins inside the mind. When we truly love, we do not judge. To love consciously and unconditionally, we must start with the self by watching how we speak and treat ourselves.

When we truly love, there is harmony and flow; there is a feeling of resonance. There is no resistance.

John Lennon famously said, "We've got this gift of love, but love is like a precious plant. You can't just accept it, leave it in the cupboard, or think it will get on by itself. You've got to keep watering it. You've got to look after it and nurture it."

Where does the desire to love and be loved come from?

We are beings of love; therefore, we all have an innate desire to love and be loved. Sometimes, when we face rejection from those individuals with whom we should be finding solace, comfort and security, our perception of love becomes distorted. Consequently we shield ourselves so as not to experience pain, and so often become numb.

Why do our thought patterns and our behavioral habits influence our ability to manifest true love and success in any area of life?

Every thought has a vibration that ripples into the cosmos and returns to us as truth, which manifests as our reality. This is why our thoughts must focus on what we want to manifest in our lives rather than past pain or situations we find disturbing. It's a major shift in your mindset and we need to protect it. For this reason, I choose not to watch the news. I prefer to create an amazing, uplifting, abundant and joy-filled reality for myself than fill my mind with the sadness and despair so often portrayed in the media.

How can we release our attachment to dysfunctional, often unconscious habits and create space for abundance and for our heart's deepest desires to become a reality?

It's a matter of transforming our mindset with conscious effort and a willingness to believe that we are worthy of living the most extraordinary life imaginable. I also use many tools in my life to help others on this path to transformation.

Becoming loving toward oneself can be one of the most challenging life commitments. It's easy to love a vulnerable and innocent baby, and it's easy to love a person who agrees with our ideals. However, it is not easy to love those who question our actions, which reflect our imperfections; in particular, it can be very challenging to love the Self, to recognize who we truly are – imperfect, damaged and dysfunctional.

It is challenging because acknowledgment of our story is important, yet constantly reliving that past story stops us from moving forward. We become fixated on the wrong that was done to us, which becomes the reason we stagnate and lose sight of that light, the truth of who we really are.

I believe we come into this world choosing our life path and the painful lessons we endure. I think we come to earth in a physical body, so our soul has the opportunity to grow through life's hardships. The way our soul grows is to see the imperfection all around us and yet, able to let go, love and forgive. We are all going through this progression and opportunity to grow together. The cycles in life can be calm or turbulent, and we all experience both ends of the scale, which side we stay on depends on our ability to master our mindset.

I met my husband after an incredibly traumatic, vulnerable time in my life.

I was 22, disempowered and he was the first man I'd met with whom I felt safe; he was a male friend who apparently didn't want anything more from me than friendship.

Until he did.

I was a young, insecure girl who had never been empowered with boundaries, living without parents and often homeless from 14, so I couldn't speak my truth and tell my newfound 35yr old male friend I only wanted friendship. I was unsure of my mindset and choices at the time. So we began to date and we later married.

Moving forward ten years into my marriage, with two beautiful daughters, nine and ten years old and a successful Naturopathic clinic, I realized I was deeply unhappy in my marriage, depressed and seeking something more.

And more turned up.

I happened to meet a man who had been living down the road from me since I'd moved to the area five years earlier, though we'd never crossed paths before.

I needed a paddock for my horses to graze and one of the ladies from our regular neighborhood morning teas suggested I ask her son. So I was riding my horse to his property. On the way down, he happened to be driving home. He pulled up alongside me, wound his window down and introduced himself. My heart skipped a beat and I suddenly felt a spark of joy within me that I hadn't known was possible.

I desperately wanted to get to know this gorgeous man on a deeper level. And sure enough, after riding together and getting to know each other, we began a very passionate love affair.

It was the only thing that brought me happiness.

And then my husband found out – I wasn't hiding it very well. This was probably a self-sabotaging move, because I knew I needed to leave my husband but I couldn't find the courage to do it.

Even after being discovered, I still couldn't find the courage I needed. Finally, I ended the affair and decided to stay in my marriage. I was remorseful because I'd cheated and hurt my husband. Nobody deserves to be hurt that way. I thought if I could become the best version of myself and heal my wounds, I could accept my husband no matter what. Sadly, I was denying myself my true feelings. I was simply trying to justify to myself why I should stay married.

But just because I was denying my feelings didn't mean they were gone. My healthy routines went out the window and my mindset slipped into drinking excessively. I started smoking again, and basically checked out of my life physically, emotionally and mentally. This is how I tolerated living a life that felt like a lie. I wasn't in love with my husband. I was going through the motions of being a good wife and mother, always sacrificing myself for the benefit of everyone else. That's what a good woman does, right?

Wrong!

One night after a couple of wines, I decided to drive to the local petrol station to buy cigarettes.

On the way to the station, I was driving around a bend in the road, probably driving too fast; I can't remember to be honest.

I went to change the song on the radio and my car veered off the road and hit a large rock, which flipped my Toyota Land Cruiser.

As my car was rolling in what felt like slow motion, I knew exactly what was happening.

What went through my mind was an acceptance that I might die. In fact, I wanted to die.

The only thing that had brought me happiness, my neighbor, my escape, was no longer in my life. And it didn't matter how much I wished my husband would change or my marriage would improve; it just wasn't going to happen. So dying seemed like a good way out.

After a right-hand nosedive into the road and a complete 360-degree flip, my car eventually stopped. I was covered with glass, and the car's roof had hit my head, removing a good portion of my hair and scalp on impact.

I was able to exit the car, despite my concussion and extreme disorientation. Within minutes a passerby came to assist.

The accident was horrific; my car was written off as a total loss. I was told by all who saw it after the accident that there was no way the driver could have survived this crash.

But what disturbed me the most was that I did survive. The disappointment scared me so much that I finally decided to change.

This was my sledgehammer. My wake-up call. I was finally ready to act and shift my mindset forever.

I still decided to stay married because I wasn't in the headspace to disrupt my life or my girl's lives or to make any big life-changing decisions.

I knew I needed to seriously work on my well-being, state of mind and happiness first and then make decisions from a healthy, grounded place.

It was time to heal and transform myself.

After my accident, I began practicing and studying in depth a style of yoga know as Kundalini that involves specific meditations that changes your brain chemistry. One of the meditations is called "Meditation for Habituation and Addiction." I was finally able to quit the bad habits that weren't serving me – sugar, alcohol, and cigarettes – along with a mental dialogue that was negative, critical and full of guilt. In my continued education as a Naturopath, I became very interested in the gut/mind connection. I healed my digestive system with microbiome testing and dietary changes, which brought balance to all areas of my body and mind.

At the end of 2018 I embarked on a journey to the United Kingdom, where I learned to teach a style of empowerment known as "soft power." So not only did I learn the techniques to come fully into my conscious, receptive, divine feminine to heal my wounding, but I became qualified to pass this wisdom and these tools on to many women.

This system I offer is holistic, enabling you to master your mindset and manifest your true values, bringing you home to your authentic, beautiful self and guaranteed to create a life of health and happiness for yourself. It's wonderful when we can come to a place of understanding ourselves on many levels, as we are complex beings with unlimited potential.

My yogic teachings indicate that there are ten bodies that co-exist within each individual. The second, third, and fourth of these are directly related to the mind, and are what I'd like to focus on here. (The other seven bodies are spoken about in my book *Awaken to Transformation*, which can be purchased at www.raisingvibrationsyoga.com.au.)

The second body is the *negative mind*, which is about the longing to belong.

The negative mind is fantastic in that it is very protective. However, if the negative mind is too strong, or over-protective, it can stop us from moving forward in our lives at all. When we acquire discernment, we can move forward safely again.

A negative mind out of balance causes us to become quite needy and often over-emotional. In addition, it can keep us stuck in fear. It can cause us to be antagonistic and unrealistic.

This might make us feel that we must be everything to everyone, often creating open relationships and disappointment. The need to be needed is powerful. However, the disappointment also intensifies, leading to a pessimistic attitude and irritating those close to us and ourselves.

Balancing the negative mind is generally accomplished through spiritual discipline. When it is balanced, we become secure within ourselves, confident in our energetic space and respect the space of others. We become valued as loyal friends, and we also become natural mediators. We become able to see both sides of the story.

Rather than longing to belong, we must long to be.

The Third Body is the *positive mind.* If the positive mind isn't used in balance, it can reinforce the negative mind. You often come across people who are very negative all the time; they dwell in their negativity and they think their negativity is fine, it's just happened to them. They've become martyrs or victims. Often their positive mind reinforces what their negative mind believes, because the positive mind isn't being used or channeled correctly.

With an unbalanced positive mind, we tend to negate ourselves. We become hesitant, uncertain and very easily manipulated. We also find it challenging to appreciate ourselves, and we have self-doubt, moodiness and maybe even depression.

A balanced Positive Mind enables us to rise to any challenge. It enables us to see others as a reflection of ourselves, allowing us to grow as balanced human beings.

We also can see the positive side of every situation.

How we see each situation in our lives is a choice. We can look to grow from it, or become a victim of circumstance.

The positive mind, when balanced, feels that there should be equality for all. Uplifting, encouraging and enthusiastic toward others brings happiness into our lives.

The fourth Body is the *neutral mind.*

The neutral mind, when balanced, takes us beyond duality. When the neutral mind is out of balance, we become indecisive, close-minded, opinionated, dogmatic, argumentative and judgmental.

However, when it is balanced, we don't have an attachment to anything and can move beyond the notion of simple duality. It lets us accept that everything is outside of our control and everything is just how it should be.

A neutral mind brings wisdom, and wisdom informs our decisions.

Our motivation is guided by compassion.

No matter what the circumstances, we understand that life lessons are what they are, and we should have no judgment. We have the wisdom and the insight to appreciate life and the lessons that life teaches us.

We become peacemakers because we come from a compassionate place. We are not attached to anything.

Suppose you are in a position where you don't know what to do or say, or you feel you may move into a negative mindset and possibly reactive state. There is a technique you can use to engage your neutral mind. When we engage our neutral mind we bring our positive and negative minds into balance. It's all about using your breath - Inhale deeply, hold your breath for nine seconds, allow your unbiased mind to review both sides of the situation from all bodies, and allow yourself to be guided by this framework. Exhale and you will come to a place where you respond rather than react.

Learning to deep breathe is a way to relax and potentially heal the nervous system.

Throughout my 23 years in clinical practice, I have come to realize that the most crucial mastery tools are self-love and empowerment techniques. We can accomplish anything in life when we acknowledge our worth as individuals and embrace a complete mindset. I've helped my clients and students come to know themselves and appreciate their imperfect paths as a means to grow and learn to nourish themselves. To let go of expectations and become one with this beautiful journey we call life.

When our mind questions a relationship, we must always come back to the point where we are questioning our relationship with self.

What is being reflected in me at this moment?

Our relationships change according to our mindset patterns. This is often termed self-sabotage – when our mindset and, therefore, behavior push a person away because we don't value ourselves enough to maintain a high-caliber long-term relationship. Relationship failure or unhappiness within a relationship always stems back to self-worth. True self-worth and the ability to communicate our needs consciously.

To be able to communicate our needs consciously, we must know what we want from a relationship. The way to discover this is first to watch our relationship with our own self. This all stems back to our thoughts and actions toward the self.

I spent a very long life self-loathing and was highly self-critical. I am aware of where this mindset came from. I had a couple of teachers who influenced me, along with a parent who was very heavily in their negative mind and unable to create healthy boundaries for me as a child. There is no blame here – this is my old story. Acknowledging these truths helps me understand myself and move forward.

What's essential in growth, healing, and living an abundant life is acknowledging we are all imperfect. As we become more aware as individuals, it becomes easier to forgive and let go of the circumstances that weren't ideal throughout our childhood and teen years.

As human beings, judgment is a very normal mental process. Being able to discern the way we judge is what matters. Have you heard the term "constructive criticism?" It's the only criticism we should allow into our lives, whether toward self or another. It's an awareness about ourselves and understanding where our behavior isn't creating harmony.

How do we judge from a place of love?

We speak the kind truth from the heart and talk to the other person's heart. This becomes a gift. The heart's energy is activated when feelings are effectively integrated into a conversation. When something goes unnoticed that isn't serving self or another and is brought to our attention, we now have the ability to change and grow and move along the path of becoming the best version of ourselves.

Create a clear vision for yourself and your life and allow yourself to feel the desire to fulfill that vision, then align yourself with the flow of that vision. Remember, flow is a deep engagement in the day-to-day journey to fulfillment. May your new mindset be full of passion and purpose. May your new story be wonderful.

You've got to win in your mind before you win in your life."

~ John Addison

CHAPTER TEN

Changing Negative Situations into Positive Outcomes

By Alexandra Tröstel

I don't have the terminology of a spiritual healer, but I do have a story to share. A story that will hopefully be a motivational one, relatable and make you believe in your dreams! Above all it's a story to help you master your mindset.

What is mindset? "A set of attitudes or fixed ideas that somebody has that are often difficult to change."

Mindsets affect and impact how we see and live our lives. Our attitude, behaviour, and actions towards an idea, an experience, and how we shift and navigate between emotions is the key to mastering our minds in a positive way.

I've learned that there are three kinds of Mindsets in my life. I'm still mastering the art of positive thinking.

The three mindsets are: *Abundance Mindset, Positive Mindset* and *Growth Mindset*. All I believe to be possessed and practiced by someone with a positive outlook on life, an optimist, someone willing to take a chance on a thought, a concept, on a moment that lights that light bulb up in your mind, instead of thinking or assuming it would never work out. By directing our thoughts and positive beliefs, we can succeed at whatever we set our mind on achieving.

I am a positive person, I'm a doer, a creator, a chaser of goals, driven. If I say I'm going to do something, I do it. It may take some time in doing it, but I always do what I say I will do in the hope that my daughter, family and friends see that and feel encouraged to do the same.

It's so easy to go through life just existing, going with the flow. Working to pay bills instead of working to fulfill our lives with meaning and purpose. We forget to elevate ourselves, to contribute to our personal and spiritual growth, to want and seek abundance. To master the way we think in order to create the life that we truly wish. To consciously make an effort on a daily basis to live the life we want to live. Overcoming limiting thoughts play a pivotal role in what we want to achieve.

We master our mindset by thinking and using positive words in our everyday life. Using positive affirmations, manifesting constantly, believing we can succeed trying something, even if we fail. We owe it to ourselves to try. Having faith in what we do, believing in ourselves can sometimes be hard. It takes courage, and our ego can shut us down, and make us doubt ourselves, but the feeling of success is elevating!

Succeeding at something we do, the feeling of accomplishment, looking back at something we have accomplished and thinking "wow, I made or did that!" The sense of making something with your own hands that people want to buy is just out of this world! The Mindset towards our success when we put our thoughts into action is measured by our own achievements, not by how we compare ourselves to others, or by the pressure others put on us to succeed or fail.

One of my favourite sayings by Erin Hansen is "But what if I fall? Oh, but my darling, what if you fly?" It is the difference between taking a chance and forever wondering what could have been. I can't live to wonder; I'd rather fail than wonder. But, on the other hand, I don't know how not to take a chance. I've often been asked whether I am taking on too much. But it's just how I work.

As a family, we migrated to Australia in 1985 and my life changed. All our lives changed. I was so lonely. The streets were so quiet, not at all what I was used to. In Chile, all the kids were out playing soccer, riding bikes, roller skating, etc., for hours after school.

We left all our family and friends behind for a better life for us. It was courageous of my parents! Such a positive and hopeful mindset. We left Chile hoping for a better life, a better education, and better possibilities. My dad Willy had a repairs business, but due to an accident, he lost it all. So he went bankrupt and had to start over again, but my parents decided they would do it in Australia if they had to start again. I'm so grateful to them for thinking in a positive way instead of thinking it was never going to work out and miss out on an opportunity to live amazing lives. They mastered their mindset by shifting the way they thought and took a leap of faith!

We didn't speak English, just the basics, like "this is a pencil," "this is a chair." It was the basic English that was taught in English class in Chile. Not enough to hold a conversation. My eldest brother and I went to an intensive English centre, but my youngest brother was three years old at the time, so he picked it up fast. At first, I didn't want to learn English, or live in Australia, but inevitably, I had to overcome the way I felt about such a huge change in our lives or be miserable. Being a teenager in a strange world was hard enough.

As a growing young adult, I took my time getting my life together, and I was happy to travel, work hard, and achieve promotions, fall in love and be someone important to someone. Some relationships taught me love, patience, self-respect, boundaries, communication, compromising, and letting go. There is so much to learn about ourselves in a relationship. What we want, what we expect, how we want to be loved and how we allow others to treat us. Unfortunately, I was involved with abusive men, physically and mentally, so I learned the hard way not to fall for the same type of man again. Had I not shifted my mindset and learned from my experiences, I would have continued to be attracted by men that didn't treat me well.

I learned about important boundaries with someone in particular I had been seeing for a while. Someone I thought I could trust. How to say NO and mean NO. I had similar situations and repeated patterns like this in my life. A lesson I needed to learn so the pattern wasn't repeated. We are in charge of how we feel and what we accept from others.

I don't need a man to fulfill or validate me, but I want to love, to share, to communicate with, and feel supported and support them in return. Unfortunately, sometimes couples are not on the same page. When one person shuts down and doesn't communicate it's impossible to know how they are feeling. I must be told what is wrong or what needs to be fixed. I can't read between the lines. If we don't know, we can't fix problems.

Sometimes our mindset is that love should be enough, but love alone is not enough for a healthy and lasting relationship, it simply isn't. Love to me, needs communication, emotion, to be vulnerable, to compromise, to listen, to be heard with no fear. Relationships are complex but not impossible - an important lesson confirmed even lately. I'm still learning to love, to be loved. My partner of seven years and I are still learning to love and be loved. It's a learning and compromising lifelong lesson. Couples don't make it to 90 years old together by chance. It takes a determined mindset.

As a mother, I did it all. I had my daughter in my mid 30's. A miracle, as I was told that with all my ovarian issues, I may never be able to fall pregnant. I was diagnosed with early cervical cancer at just 21-years-old, but it was detected early and was treated. I looked after my baby daughter, my partner, the dog, and the house. I cleaned, washed, cooked, shopped for groceries, walked the dog, and never took time for myself, even when my baby slept. I would prepare dinner, iron, set the table, etc. I felt the need to have it all ready by the time my partner came home, a very old-fashioned South American custom that had been passed down to me.

So many of us mothers don't permit ourselves to be anything else, not that being a mum isn't a full-time and wonderful labour of love, please don't get me wrong, there is nothing wrong with wanting to be a stay-at-home mum. We sometimes feel guilty or judged that we are not dedicating enough time or our all to our children, partners, and home. Our parents and family have different mindsets about what we should be doing and how. We get the "by this time, I was feeding you meat or chicken or making meals from scratch," etc. We have to be true to ourselves; what worked for our parents may not work for us. We are not disappointing them by not doing what they did. It's choosing what works for us.

My mindset at the time was that I feared failing others and I had to do everything in the house, and music was not a priority. However, the wonderful thing is, we can do both, nurture our kids, our partners, our homes AND nurture ourselves. More and more women are empowering themselves by having a small business, working from home, and permitting themselves to be something other than a wonderful, dedicated mum and wife - a positive mindset movement from a new generation's perspective. I have amazing, loving mum friends that have businesses working from home; they have been a true inspiration to overcome their fears and chase their goals.

Music has always been such a big part of my life. At school, I started playing drums in year 9, then gradually concentrated on singing until year 12. Still, I had been so scared to do so since then, for the fear of not being good enough and comparing myself to people and friends that had been singing all their lives. But, of course, my comparison was unrealistic. I was also teaching myself to play the guitar for a couple of years on and off before I had my beautiful daughter, but I put that aside until she was three years old, when my relationship with her dad ended in 2011.

Then my daughter and I moved out and into a lovely, small apartment in the heart of Mortdale, NSW, and I had more time to pick up the guitar. After many years of not playing, I brought the joy of music back into my life. The new mindset then was that I could do both, make my daughter happy and myself. Happy mum, happy child. Overcoming limiting beliefs about feeling guilty about doing something that made me happy. I shifted the guilt into a happy emotion.

I was working three days a week as a secretary in Mortdale. Our childcare centre was right behind our building, I could see it out of the apartment window. I had wished for a new home where everything was close together, work and day-care and that's how it came to be. I imagined and pictured in my head what I needed to start anew. By overcoming the fear of having to start over again, I saw it as a positive opportunity. I could have stayed living unhappily, but that would have robbed us all of a happy life. I decided to be strong for a better future.

I was singing and playing guitar more often, learning more chords as constantly as possible, and I started writing songs, songs that people, family, and friends liked. Songs I was proud of came from a place of my own experiences. And they weren't half bad! A producer even used one of the songs in a film of his.

Shifting my fear into happiness was a major mindset adjustment, as I was learning to feel confident and not compare myself to artists that had been singing and playing guitar since they were five-years-old.

One day I felt comfortable and confident enough to post my first song on Facebook in 2019 and everyone loved it. I felt so happy and accomplished. Not because of the lovely supportive and encouraging comments I received, but because I did it! I faced my fear and it paid off. By overcoming limiting beliefs again, I uploaded a song, without being negative about what the outcome could be.

I had the opportunity to record and release a single on Facebook and YouTube in 2018 with the excellent, highly recommended, multi-talented musician/producer Andro Martinez from "Martinez Productions" in Earlwood, NSW. The song is called "Heaven Bound" https://youtube.com/watch?v=3sjVygOnOCU&feature=share, a song about two old friends randomly bumping into each other on the street, catching up regularly, and sharing similar life experiences. They start to connect and fall in love. I have so many songs written; I think we are all capable of writing our stories and feelings into something beautiful if we put our minds to it.

Life begins at a crossroads because I really believe that when we are confronted by a dead end in life, such as heartbreak, loss, grief, having to change jobs, etc., we cannot remain stagnant. If we do, we get stuck in a rut, we feel sorry for ourselves, and create a negative environment. But, while at a crossroads, if we look at it positively, we get to make choices. We swim, or we sink. We get a chance to reinvent ourselves, to create a new path, we can turn a negative situation into a positive one. If we look at new beginnings with a positive mindset, it's exciting!

By exercising the "Growth mindset" we can try a different approach. Growth mindset; believing that through hard work and positive strategies, we can achieve a positive outcome.

A crucial moment in my life happened when I worked for an over-friendly boss, whose hands ended up on my neck when we went for a drive looking for new products. I could have put up with it out of fear of standing up for myself. Still, I would have been disrespecting myself and sending the wrong message to my boss that inappropriate behaviour was tolerated or accepted. We argued,

I got my bags and I left. I was left with no income just a month before Christmas, a very stressful time, but an important lesson about BOUNDARIES.

I didn't want to seek assistance from the government, I was too proud, but I had bills to pay as a single parent. So, I went to apply for financial assistance from one of the government offices in Sydney. There was a notice board that read, "Do you have a business idea?" I thought to myself, I have so many! A light bulb in my head went wild with so many ideas that I could bring to reality with assistance and financial support. My mindset then was to persevere and be my own boss, to make something of an idea, my concept that I could bring to life. The ideas I had were original and unique; there was nothing like it in the marketplace. I saw an opportunity and I grabbed it with both hands. I wasn't going to let my ex-boss make me a victim.

The concept that I had thought of was to create something that helped showcase a specific product on a window by a business – a Point Of Sale product, (POS). Working as a window merchandiser I saw the need for such a product. But, unfortunately, there was nothing like it on the market.

I started collecting wooden pallets from the side of the road, and I also approached local businesses that no longer needed them, making it an environmentally friendly product.

My dad, the fantastic handyman he is, had lots of tools he no longer used. He lent me his circular saw cutter, and I started purchasing my own devices for my little business, and I started creating! I converted my garage into my workshop. It was full of life, positive vibes, and prospects.

I built a rustic wooden lightbox. A hollow frame with a light inside to highlight a product or products in shop windows. I made a prototype and I was in awe of what I had just made!! Growing up, I saw my dad make and fix things, and out of pure curiosity, I taught myself woodwork. As a result, I've always been hands-on with home repairs, DYIs, interior decorating projects, etc.

I now needed a business name. I thought long and hard about a name that could be different, unique, and engaging which also reflected me a little. Finally, I came up with "Gypsy at Heart." I've always loved and worn long skirts, bell-bottom jeans, lacey tops, bangles, big earrings, and long hair. My friends say I have a hippy, boho style.

I started the business course in November 2019. I was so excited about the prospect of starting my own small business and learning all the aspects of running a company. I went to class in between school hours, I met many outstanding people with ideas and concepts they, too, wanted to bring to life, people with similar goals. They too mastered their mindset in order to create a life for themselves, overcoming doubt, fear, and believing they could make a difference in their lives.

I hand-made a number of Rustic Light Boxes in stock and started approaching florists and home boutique-style businesses. By the beginning of December, I had sold more than 15 rustic light boxes ! I was on a roll. Then I thought of another product using the same concept of the light box, only with a hanger to hang a pot plant inside, a popular item with Florists. I got mum and her beautiful macrame skills involved in this product. She is also very creative. It was exhilarating and promising! Determination and thinking positively, I shifted the way I thought and I was creating things businesses were valuing and using in their windows.

My beautiful, soulful friend Catherine Kavadas had seen my Rustic Plant Holders and asked if I could make her some that would hold two bottles of wine. I loved the idea and made a prototype. Catherine and her husband Alex both loved it. Her husband has a business called "Mr Handyfix." He specialises in home repair services to homes and apartments through real estate offices around

Sydney. They wanted to give their clients something special and different for Christmas, so the Rustic Wine Holder concept was born. I was in such a happy, creative stage in my life again!

However, then came massive news of a virus taking over the world, a virus we knew very little about called Covid-19! It was something no one saw coming. We knew nothing about it, just that it affected the whole world. Shops and businesses began to close down due to lockdown rules, and so my products stopped selling. My business had come to a halt after just gaining some momentum. These were dark times for many.

I found myself worried and stressed about how to pay bills yet again, so my brain was working overtime, working out what the next step would be with a business I had just taken off the ground but couldn't sell my products to closed-down shops! I didn't want to fall into despair and doubt. I knew if I kept my positive mindset, I would be fine.

Many years earlier, I dated someone who made drawings, paintings, and sculptures. I had kept an empty bottle of a Chilean drink called Pisco at home in the shape of a "Moai" statue brought back by my parents on one of their trips to Chile. I asked my then-boyfriend to make a statue of the Moai bottle for the garden. He made his version of one. We showed family and friends and they loved them, so we began to make them and sell them to our Chilean family and friends.

We broke up due to infidelity and mentally abusive issues. Another lesson I learned is how I don't want to be treated by a partner. For another two years, I kept making them on my own, my version of the Moais until I had to move houses and I no longer had enough room to make them.

Fast forward to 2020, I've always been proud of my home, even though I rent. I fixed the back garden into a cosy little Oasis full of flowers, I planted yuccas, and put lights up surrounding the fence, and put some photos on Facebook that included the Moai I had kept even after all these years, I wasn't showcasing it. It was part of the photo. One of my friends asked where I had bought the Moai. I said I had made it, but many years ago. My friend replied if I ever make them again, she would love to buy one. Another light bulb went off in my head, however, I had many unresolved negative issues connected to the Moais because of the toxic relationship with my ex. Still, I thought it was time to resolve these issues. By changing my mindset surrounding the unresolved negative issues, I consciously made an effort to overcome the past and turned it into a positive journey full of possibilities.

I sat long and hard with the idea, and even though it had been more than 12 years since I had carved, I started intentionally letting go of some of the pain still attached to the Chilean Moai. Of course, it wasn't an overnight process. I had decided that I wanted to start carving again, which meant beginning to let go of the negativity to make something positive in my life from a bad experience! By mastering my mindset, I had another chance of reinventing myself and the business.

I researched where to source the material to hand carve and bought a block. It was late one evening and I started reconnecting to the craft. It took me more than five hours to carve it. As I remembered how to shape the Moai, old wounds resurfaced, but I almost forgot as I was in a deep carving trance.

When I finished carving the Moai, I got a strong sense of self-achievement, not just because I could carve again, but also because I began letting go of old memories and releasing old scars. I saw a new beginning!

I posted pictures of my Moais and the inquiries started coming in!! I had just reinvented myself, Gypsy at Heart, and began fulfilling orders for friends and family in the Latin community in Australia.

"La Previa Radio Show 2.0" is a live Facebook radio program on Wednesday evenings led and hosted by the beautiful Angelica

Mansilla, a program that highlights the incredible works of Latin artists and musicians.

I had heard the program many times while I was making dinner and loved the connection and vibe the hosts had and the South American music they played, and I started following them weekly.

During one program, I sent a comment to say hi to the hosts and I jokingly said they needed a Moai as a prop on the set of the radio. They replied, saying they would have to find one. I responded with "I make them!" I saw an opportunity and I took the chance to say "I will make one for you."

A few weeks later, Angelica invited me to the radio studio as a guest. Angelica had seen my Facebook positive vibes posts, my songs, and my art. That's when I took them the Moai I made as a gift. The interview was amazing. They loved the Moai and I got to sing my original song "Heaven Bound" live on air! The response was overwhelming towards my song and the Moai.

From that experience, I started believing more in myself. I believed I made something of myself from negative experiences and so I wanted to passionately keep sharing my story to inspire and motivate others to do the same. About a year later I was lucky enough to be invited by Angelica to regularly co-host on La Previa Radio 2.0!! Another amazing experience I've been fortunate to live! La Previa is a program very much loved by the Latin community.

Believe in yourself, be determined, take that step to create an opportunity! That is again mastering the way you see things. The difference between taking the initiative or passing it, in fear of failing.

During the radio interview, I was invited to take part in a South American event "Holding Hands Sin Fronteras" organised by the lovely *Jechi Cecilia Jimenez*. I felt honoured to be invited to an event showcasing so many amazing artists and musicians in the Latin community. I made 20 Moais and sold them all - another memorable part of my journey. I was nervous and questioned if I could do it as it was the first event I took part as Gypsy at Heart, and it was amazing!

Not long after that event, the sweet *Luisa Caroca Lucero* asked me to participate in her live Facebook radio program "Conversando con Luisa" during the pandemic. It was a wonderful and warm Facebook program she set up from her own home to keep the Latin Community connected during the lockdown showcasing and interviewing amazing Latin musicians, artists and small businesses in Sydney and some live from Chile. So many businesses were born during the pandemic by amazing people with the mindset and vision to reinvent themselves to survive during lonely lockdown months. I showcased my Moais and my song.

I've been so fortunate to be supported by so many strong, empowered women friends and family, in these last few years! The beautiful and kind Milena-Ben David also showcased my Moais in her NSW SLASA "Summer Serenades" project. She brought traditional music, art, and gifts to the Latin community after the Covid-19 lockdowns through her unique events.

The delightful Tracey Bahamondez is another empowered woman who has also mastered her mindset, and is doing marvelous things. She works so hard organising so many wonderful events "Eventos Latinos" for the Latin Community. Tracey, overcoming doubt and fear, has been immensely supportive of my art.

Another empowered woman, my very good friend *Nancy Mattos* is an amazing spiritual healer and a wonderful bilingual wedding celebrant. Nancy approached me to start our very own program on a Saturday night during the pandemic lockdowns to keep the musicians and our Latin community connected. The music industry was hit hard by Covid-19, so she was unable to work for two years. Nancy and I went live on air via zoom interviewing different musicians every Saturday evening for 12 weeks, from 7pm to almost 9pm. The artists sang live via zoom in their homes, so many people connected to our program. We were always left on a high at the end, bringing music, joy, fun, and laughter each Saturday night during what were dark times for many. What a fantastic experience.

As the lockdowns eased, our program came to a close. But on the last program, I was so sad that we wouldn't be able to continue, and support musicians that I thought of a house concert that would still be able to help musicians while the lockdowns started to ease. We still had no idea what life would look like after lockdowns.

My concept was to have a small and cosy group of amazing people in my backyard, decorate it with some fairy lights, candles, cosy blankets, and pillows, to support our local Latin musicians, and also support food businesses by having their food for sale on the night.

The ticket price went to the artists and the food sales were kept by the caterers. Because the event was in the open air of my backyard, I named it "AireLibre Backyard Sessions" meaning "open-air backyard sessions." I did the first one and it was a hit! I had so much support from artists, caterers and the people that came to the events. I organised four more events in the space of a year! One every three months. All the events supporting artists and food caterers. It took hard work to organise. Look for an artist, find a caterer, and coordinate both for the same night, sell tickets, marketing and social media promotion on all platforms, maintain the grass, set up tables, chairs, and the decoration to make sure it was looking wow, take pictures and videos on the night to promote it. But I was driven, I did it all to help, to see people have an amazing time at night, to fill my backyard full of wonderful vibes.

Another amazing industry I have worked hard to get into is the TV/Film industry. By pursuing a wish, I was so determined to look for a reputable agent. I did the research; I went to a few interviews and I found one. I believed I could be a part of this amazing industry, I saw myself making commercials again.

Just prior to the second wave of Covid-19, I had the amazing chance to be an extra in a major Marvel Film, Thor, Love & Thunder. That was such a great experience! Filming on different days at different times over four weeks. Some nights we finished filming at 3am. My beautiful mum Beatriz helped me look after my daughter Macy. So I'd get home at 4am, sleep for two hours, get up, get ready, take my daughter to school, and go to work. Then, at 4:00 pm, I had to be back on set for another 12-hour shoot. I have since worked on a TV commercial and I just finished filming on another feature film, but, due to confidentiality agreements, I can't name yet, but it's been amazing to be a part of it too. I'm looking forward to many more opportunities.

Then came another brilliant opportunity! To write a chapter in this amazing book "*A Journey of Riches – Master Your Mindset*." I didn't have to think twice. It's a once-in-a-lifetime opportunity to share my experience of this scale! I'm so grateful to John Spender! If my personal journey can influence, inspire you and others to have a positive mindset, to master it in a way that you look at life in a positive light, then it will all be worth it.

Believe that you can achieve anything. It's not easy stepping out of your comfort zone, don't go into anything thinking that it won't work and fuel that idea with doubt. Follow your dreams and goals and compromise in your relationships. They are not easy but fight for your love, live life, and make your life count! Remember with any ending comes a new beginning, a new lesson. Master your mindset and see an end as a new beginning.

You can do anything you want, if you work hard to get it and dedicate yourself. Look at your resources; When, what, how, and where. A positive mindset is required for everything you want to achieve. Thoughts and actions that will fuel your goals, not hinder them. There are so many wonderful books to inspire you, including this one, and so many inspiring videos available on the internet.

Live your life with purpose, with full intent. Pick up that instrument you have always wanted to learn to play, pick up a paintbrush and learn to paint. Take up Salsa or Tango lessons, start meditating, do yoga, get a new job, write a chapter in a book. Whatever it is, small or big, do it with the thought that your life will be richer.

Live each day and fill it with fun, hopes, and dreams. Life is not just about working long hours to pay bills. We don't take our cars and houses with us. There is so much more to life! If we positively master our mindset, we can achieve what we wish, big or small, if we manifest what we want, direct our thoughts to a positive place, and have the courage to take a leap of faith. Then, you will live your life fully!

"When you master your mindset, you free yourself to achieve the level of success you desire."

~ Unknown

CHAPTER ELEVEN

The Power of a Positive Mindset

By John Spender

The human mind is something that has boggled scientists and philosophers for centuries. Our brain, which is made up of every type of mental phenomena, such as our thoughts, memory, willpower, sensation, emotions, and intellect. The mind is so intricate that we still don't know much about it, despite it being one of the most studied organs of the human body.

One frequently asked question when it comes to the mind is, "Why do we do the things we do?" It is, no doubt, a difficult question to answer. Why does one struggle to stop eating a whole box of cookies while someone else might not even have an appetite for sweets? Why is one person good at organization while another can't seem to remember how to complete the most basic task?

Of course, everyone is unique and various health conditions might come into play when we discuss the differences between people. But sometimes, pushing ourselves to reach our full potential comes down to "mastering our mindset."

"Mastering your mindset" is a phrase that has grown in popularity over the recent years, and people claim to be changing their lives in all areas by gaining control over their thoughts. However, mastering our mindset isn't something that happens overnight. For most of us, it's a continual process that will require dedication and hard work for the rest of our lives, but by slowly building up the tools necessary to change your perspective, you can change your life for the better.

So in this chapter, I want to discuss the areas where I have learned to master my mindset and build a better life for myself.

I was a real go-getter in my twenties. No matter my situation, I always found the positive in the negative. I worked in the landscaping industry for years and started my first business when I was twenty. No matter the challenge, I work toward a solution. I still remember the first large landscaping contract I won. I had been reading Richard Branson's autobiography *Losing my Virginity and* began adapting Richards's philosophy of saying yes and figuring out the how later. Even though I had never worked on a project of this magnitude, I said yes first with the goal of figuring out the "how" later. It worked! There is power in starting with a positive can-do attitude that breeds confidence and belief.

I eventually went on to build a team of 15, not including hired contractors. The initial challenge was the pressure and my lack of ability to release that pressure. I found that being responsible for managing my team and making sure the projects were completed on time was stressful. On top of this, evidently there were mistakes. For example, when one of the boys put a back roe through a water pipe, it flooded the job site in minutes. Then there is the pressure of meeting project completion dates. If they're not met then payments are delayed and it can be a strain on resources to pay wages. Looking back in reflection, having a hobby or sport would have helped. But everything happens for a reason and my meltdown led me to the root cause of the issue.

Unresolved trauma. This is a problem we know much more about today than in the late nineties. In that era, people kept their therapy sessions a secret and many considered seeking help a weakness. My mindset back then was to sweep the emotionally significant events of my childhood under the rug. There was the incident of having my face rubbed into my own feces that had fallen onto the floor as I ran to the bathroom when I was seven. The incident was never spoken of again and it had a profound impact on me. It heavily affected my mental state, especially when under pressure.

My positive mindset was weighed down by an anchor of negative coping mechanisms triggered by my increased workload. Recreational drugs and partying became my way of self-medicating my emotional wounds. One by one, I lost my major contracts and quickly spiraled out of control. Things had become so bad that I moved back in with my mom and her partner. At twenty-four, it was a shameful experience that dented my confidence and self-belief. My four years as a business owner came to a dramatic end. The positive was that I eased off the recreational drugs, gaining some semblance of control over my life again.

I started reading about unresolved trauma and how that leads to adopting a negative mindset. I was surprised by what I found. It turns out that most of us are hardwired to look for the negatives in different situations, especially if we have unresolved childhood wounds. However, even though we might be hardwired to look for the negatives, how we respond to our thoughts and feelings plays a large part in how we feel in our day-to-day lives. The articles I read and the seminars I attended mirrored my own experiences. What I read in books and learned at various personal development events confirmed that the longer I fed into a negative mindset, the harder it was to notice the positives, even if I had had an overwhelmingly positive day or experience. The past bears a heavy weight, and we need to learn to live in the present moment.

I experienced large doses of how unjust the emotional, physical, and sexual abuse was for a young child to face. Once the repressed traumas reappeared, I felt a real need to tell everyone about it, and I felt like somebody HAD TO KNOW. But the more I read about negative mindsets, the more I realized what the most essential first step in my journey to mastering my attitude had to be: healing my childhood wounds.

All sexual abuse is heinous and only serves to pass on childhood wounds from one generation to the next. After working on myself, I learned to forgive my uncle for molesting me while we were "wrestling" putting an ice cube in my bum as other family members watched and laughed. I consider myself lucky it was an isolated incident and never happened again. But the fact that the incident was never spoken of left me feeling confused and unsure about myself.

While there were many steps in my journey to creating a more positive mindset, one of the biggest ones was to stop talking about the negatives. For example, I became solution-oriented when problems arose in my life. If I had an issue with something that could be fixed, I would speak up. If I was stuck in traffic, I would listen to a positive CD about mindset and manifestation or anything uplifting and educational. Instead of dreading rush-hour traffic, I learned to enjoy the experience.

Now, I want to take a moment here to say that speaking up is essential! If you are going through a hard time, are in an abusive situation, or experiencing something that you need help with, you should absolutely say something. However, I discovered in this part of my journey that complaining about something harmless is pointless; for instance, when a client doesn't pay you and you feel the need to tell the whole world about it rather than focusing on a solution or doubling down on your efforts to do an outstanding job for the majority of clients that treat you well. Sure, we might feel the need to let loose about something every now and then, but it doesn't make us feel better in the long run and can contribute to perpetuating feelings of shame and sadness. Not to mention the likelihood of repeating the momentum of negative experiences.

Furthermore, it's important to note that talking about complex subjects like grief and depression is not the same as complaining. Therefore, it is necessary to distinguish between complaining and when an issue needs to be addressed. Finally, remember not everyone around you will feel the same way, and it's important to surround yourself with friends and mentors who support and love you no matter what you're going through.

So that was step one for me. And honestly? It was effective. When I stopped talking about everything that bothered me, it gave me time to examine what needed to be said. Sometimes I would still end up speaking up about it. Still, that would only happen when I realized the thing that was bothering me seriously needed to be addressed. I also learned a lot more about what I wanted. I realized that I often get annoyed in loud, busy spaces, like clubs. After spending some time with that thought, I discovered I value quiet, one-on-one time with my friends, and now I enjoy my outings a lot more. I'll only visit loud spaces if it's a celebration, like a birthday or a wedding, then I can prepare myself for the experience and focus on the moment instead of the overstimulation I feel from the environment.

There I was, already finding my way to a more positive life. But again, I want to stress that positive thinking doesn't mean you always have to be positive. Negative thoughts are a normal part of life; it is unhealthy to pretend they aren't. I'm not a fan of "positivity-only" spaces, and we must discuss difficult experiences and the many mental health issues many people face. However, I can't tell you how much my life improved once I began to focus on the positives in my life.

So, let's move on to the next step to mastering a negative mindset: gratitude.

When reading books or articles about changing a negative mindset, gratitude is almost always at the top of the list. So let's get into practicing it.

There are many ways you can incorporate gratitude into your life, but this is what worked for me: I kept a gratitude journal. Every day, I write down at least three things I am grateful for. Sometimes I write a lot more. These can be small things, like a delicious cookie I enjoyed, or more profound things, like watching a sunset. Practicing gratitude is proven to create a happier life and can be a great way to reset your mood if you're feeling down or upset. Every day without fail, I ask my core team what they are most grateful for before they start their workday. This simple technique creates an air of positivity before my team starts the day.

Consistency is the foundation for success with any habit, I make expressing gratitude a daily practice. One of the things I say is, "I appreciate all that I am and all that I have." Along with "I love and accept myself, just the way that I am" and "I always attract the highest and best in all people." One of the attributes of mastering your mindset is speaking your desired reality into existence.

Another way I practice gratitude is by checking in with myself throughout the day, especially during periods of frustration. For example, when one of my team members hasn't completed a task, instead of getting angry about the delay, I think about how grateful I am to have a business and how grateful I am to have a home to live in. I appreciate my good fortune in being safe and dry inside if there is rough weather. I might also use this time to put on some music or a podcast I love and appreciate the unexpected time to listen to something I enjoy on my own.

It can take some time, but practicing the mindset of gratitude has made me kinder, more patient, and, hopefully, a much more enjoyable person to be around. So I encourage you to try it.

The final tool I used and continue to use throughout my journey toward positive thinking is asking myself if my concern is paramount and if what I'm annoyed about is the thing that's bothering me.

This is an excellent tool because just taking those few extra moments to have a conversation with ourselves can help us see that the thing that's bothering us is only temporary and won't bother us thirty minutes from now. This way, when something is truly important, it will hold more weight because you'll only be bringing up the issues that truly matter instead of something that was simply a passing annoyance.

It's worth deciphering whether what's bothering you at the moment is the issue triggering you. So, for example, a lot of the problems I was having with drug addiction, I realized, were because I wasn't feeling worthy or feeling I was enough. Hence, diving deep into personal development, quitting recreational drugs altogether in 2010, and transiting out of my second landscaping company into a mindset coach and international NLP trainer helped alleviate many of the problems I had been having.

Mastering your mindset takes a lot of time and it is a constant process. There have been times when I have fallen back into old habits of thinking and victimhood, but now I can recognize what's happening and have the tools at hand to deal with those feelings when they pop back up.

Before I tell you another way that I mastered my mindset, let's revisit the tools I used to change my negative thinking into positive thinking.

1. Stop vocalizing negativity.
2. Practice gratitude.
3. Have a conversation with yourself: "Is this important? What is beyond the surface of my trigger and behavior?"

Now that I've covered how I changed my thinking from negative to positive, let's talk about how I mastered my mindset concerning my morning routine.

Many people struggle with exercise, which is one of the most common reasons why people want to learn to master their mindset. But first, let's look at what science says:

Exercise is good for you, full stop. It helps combat many severe medical conditions such as high blood pressure, depression, cancer, and strokes. It makes you feel good. It helps keep you at a good weight for your body. It makes you sleep better, it gives you more energy, the list goes on and on. So why is it so hard to do?

The reasons why many of us have trouble exercising are complex, and there isn't one straight answer. But there are many things that are good for us that we don't do, such as eating healthy. Often, it's a matter of falling in love with the process. Many people hold multiple jobs, have families to take care of, and social commitments. Sometimes it feels downright impossible to fit in a workout. I get it. So, how did I make a change?

Well, the truth is, for many years, I didn't. Instead, I spent several years bopping around at different yoga shalas, doing yoga only with the instructor I liked. I even worked at a gym for a few years in the hopes of motivating myself to get into an exercise routine, but it never stuck. I'd exercise sometimes, but it was super inconsistent.

After years of inconsistency, the global pandemic struck and, although I didn't experience any lockdown myself, my local yoga studio closed down. So I found a facilitator that I liked on YouTube. I enjoyed that I could choose the yoga routine and duration, which helped my motivation. Aided by the positive feelings I received after yoga, I began to practice longer and more often. I didn't have a problem with exercise or yoga. I had a problem with the duration and routine.

After that day, everything changed for me. I stopped seeking exercises I "should do" and started seeking activities I wanted to do. I started boxing training again with a personal trainer, hiking, and cycling. I stopped worrying about working out to look a certain way and began caring more about how I felt when my body moved. So much of the exercise didn't feel like exercising. It felt fun. And that's how I mastered the mindset. I realized that exercise isn't supposed to be boring or make you feel bad, and it's supposed to feel joyful.

Sure, if you're training to be in a superhero movie or trying to win a weightlifting competition, you'll need to do certain types of exercises to get those results. But if you're exercising because you want to stay healthy and sleep better, then it doesn't matter what you do as long as you do it. There isn't one right way to exercise, so if you're struggling to make physical activity a part of your routine, I highly encourage you to start small, figure out what you love, and don't worry about anything else.

I do want to acknowledge that not everyone has the privilege that I have to do several types of sports and activities. I get it, and I've been there. But there are many types of exercises that you can do for free! Running and walking requires a good pair of shoes. YouTube has endless videos with different workouts for you to explore, and many studios offer cheap or free trials to determine whether you like something. Some studios even offer free memberships for working a couple of shifts at the front desk. This is something I took advantage of myself when I was struggling financially in my younger years. So, don't feel like you can't find the type of exercise you love if you don't have the means. I believe there's something out there for everyone.

That's my main takeaway when it comes to exercise, and I know there is a bit of unlearning that comes with it. So many of us are conditioned to believe that our bodies are supposed to look a certain way so that we are valued in society. Still, all that matters is that we are as happy and as healthy as we can be, which will look different for everybody. When you can get past needing to look a certain way, you can listen to how your body feels when you do certain types of movement and only do the kinds that make you feel good and energetic.

Before I close this chapter, I'll leave you with one more trick. When I find myself in a moment where I struggle with exercise, I do something minimal. I turn on a song I like and dance until it's over. I go for a walk around the block. I spend two minutes stretching or doing ten minutes of yoga. While it's not much, I know that I'll feel better in the end. Doing something small that

I enjoy is much better than doing nothing. We're all human, and remember, mastering your mindset and changing your thinking takes time.

Mastering my mindset in relation to exercise has resulted in a big shift in my expectations. Sure, sometimes I do hour-long workouts, classes, or training sessions, but at other times, going out for a long walk with a podcast is exactly what my body and mind are craving. Interestingly enough, the biggest issue regarding exercising and mastering my mindset was listening to what my mind and body were trying to tell me all along.

I hope this chapter was helpful to you, and good luck on your journey. I know it's not always easy, but be kind to yourself and soon you will have more confidence in yourself and you'll start seeing positive changes.

"Once your mindset changes, everything on the outside will change along with it."

~Steve Maraboli

AUTHOR BIOGRAPHIES

Bec Bucci

CHAPTER ONE

Rebecca (Bec) Bucci is an American Board Certified Sexologist, Clinical Sexuality Coach, Global Speaker and Relationships Sexpert.

Founder of G Spot Sex Therapy Down Under, her work specialises in educating couples and individuals in all areas of taboo, sexual dysfunction and rehabilitation. Her passionate approach of inspiring women to embrace their complete sexual self and in expressing their deepest desires around pleasure have led her to be featured in international bestselling print magazines and international bestselling books as a featured Coauthor. Rebecca facilitates couples, women and men's workshops and retreats globally via face to face instruction and via the G Spot online subscription app.

Rebecca states "Becoming a Sexologist was my calling, my life's work, to open the door to acceptance of the weird, of the taboo, of the kink, of the extra-ordinary expressions we can experience whilst living through this human experience. This is my purpose to inspire all women to step fully into their femininity "now," to embrace it, allowing it to ignite by trusting it and finally by nurturing it through its many stages of maturity. ALWAYS tend to the fire within. Don't wait to become…

An unapologetically, authentically raw and real 100% woman."

Kyle Zagrodzky

CHAPTER TWO

Kyle Zagrodzky is the Founder and CEO of OsteoStrong. A serial entrepreneur, Kyle has founded several companies earning well over 100 million in revenue. He is drawn to concepts that improve the human condition.

OsteoStrong exists to deliver the highest level of physical freedom to people around the world by leveraging new scientific discoveries. With the support of Tony Robbins – himself a user of OsteoStrong technology and investor in the company – Kyle now works to bring knowledge of the best biohacks to the global marketplace.

Speaking on stages around the world, Kyle is best known for his frequent presence at Tony Robbins' events where he presents on bio-hacking and OsteoStrong. Kyle brings together many different experiences across several industries, earning a strong reputation in mid and C-level executive team development, strategic planning, manufacturing, marketing, professional sales, software development, education systems, publishing, and business coaching.

A serial entrepreneur, Kyle has more than 30 years' experience funding and launching a multitude of businesses with great success.

Kyle lives and serves his life's mission of helping others from his home in Brentwood, Tennessee along with his wife and three sons.

Dr. Olga Zabora, PsyD

CHAPTER THREE

International Best Selling Author, Speaker, Certified Master NLP Coach, NLP Trainer's Trainer holds a Doctorate Degree in Clinical Psychology from the US, Diploma of Clinical Hypnotherapy from HMI and multiple certifications including Gestalt Therapy at PGI, Jungian Analytical Psychology at Jung Institute of Los Angeles, Past Life Regression & Spiritual Regression w/ Brian Weiss.

She was a collaborating author in *Transform Your Wounds into Wisdom* is the #1 Amazon Best Seller 2022. She is getting published her own book in 2023.

Dr. Olga's extensive training both in the US and outside the country combined with 20 years of education, and experience, deep exploration of Jungian Therapy, Dream Analysis, Holotropic Breathwork®, meditation, mindfulness, yoga, Philosophical Tantra, Sacred Temple Mandala Dance in India, Multiple studies about Feminine Nature and Energy from world renown professionals.

Dr. Olga holds Certificate from Optimum Health Institute, Advanced Nutritional and Integrative Medicine for Mental Health Professionals, Shamanism from Michael Harner's Foundation, and other spiritual practices has given the opportunities to integrate her knowledge and utilize it in assisting clients with their life journeys and lasting positive changes.

Her passion lies in helping you to become aware of your own resources by bringing up the best parts of yourself to guide you gently with your conscious transformation into the best and happiest version of yourself.

Currently Dr. Olga continues publishing her books, clinical practice, coaching, teaching classes and conducting empowering women's retreats along with sharing her humor, knowledge and experience with everyone who attends her courses at www. GoddessEvent.com & drolgazabora.com

Amanda Lees

CHAPTER FOUR

Amanda Lees lives in Australia with her husband and is the proud mother of their three children. She has been a nurse for 23 years with a Bachelor of Nursing and a Post Graduate Diploma in Women's Health.

Amanda is currently studying for a Diploma in counseling while still nursing and writing. She has recently published her first book, *According to Plan – Riding the unpredictable waves of motherhood.* By publishing her book, she endeavors to inspire others and assist in their healing as she openly shares how her family navigates through Autism, ADHD, Oppositional Defiant Disorder, Obsessive Compulsive Disorder, multiple Anaphylactic food allergies, Dyslexia, Dysgraphia, Anxiety, and an array of medical conditions to now thrive in this world. Unfortunately, all topics are often kept behind closed doors.

Amanda is currently working on her next book, *Unwrapping Motherhood.* This book allows other mothers to share their stories to facilitate their healing and the readers. Revealing that all mothers have a different and unique journey. She trained in Elohim healing, combining other modalities and channeling healing energy. This process restores balance in your body, mind, and soul. Amanda has recently started her business to extend her support to others - Heart Centred Health. Her vision is to empower each individual to acknowledge and accept their own story, allowing them to thrive in this life no matter what obstacles may present themselves along the way.

FB - Amanda Lees

Insta - Accordingtoplan.amandalees

Email – Accordingtoplan.amandalees@gmail.com

Website – www.heartcentredhealth.online

Book - *According to Plan - Riding the Unpredictable Waves of Motherhood.* https://mybook.to/AccordingtoPlan

Inarra Aryane Griffyn

CHAPTER FIVE

Inarra Aryane Griffyn is a Visionary Business Guide offering a Spiritual Elixir to creatives and entrepreneurs, to help them gain expression, visibility and opportunity. She helps stimulate and enhance her client's vision so that they generate, manifest and experience luxury, at their pace, in perfect timing.

To do this, using the ancient cycles of the seasons, Moon and Solar alignments, such as the Spring Equinox or Autumn Equinox, she helps them activate new cycles of transformation. Her clients follow a series of mastery prompts, based on perfect timing to launch their products, programs and projects. Her recipe of mastery skills helps them unfold into their next level of business and life. They experience quantum transformation by following her recipe of "Luxury in harmony with Nature," and she had guided many high level business owners to reach their dream life.

Based in London UK, she teaches 11 Queens, 11 Kings Mastery Mastery Programmes online globally. She also hosts retreats such as The Mysteries of Avalon in Glastonbury, UK. Inarra is a public speaker and author of four books, the latest *The Little Book Of Influence* published in 2021. A High Priestess of Avalon she teaches ritual and the Priestess Path.

You can contact her directly by email inarra@thevisionaries.international and on her social media platforms FB & Insta @inarraaryanegriffyn @newearthvisionaries

To find out about her programs and coaching join her mailing list and receive a free ebook https://optin.thevisionaries.international/newearthvisionaries

Olga Brooks

CHAPTER SIX

Olga Brooks was born and raised in Russia. At the age of 22 in the late 90s she immigrated to the USA.

Experiencing a stroke at 27 years of age, Olga touched base with death and supernatural experiences. Which laid the back road to her spiritual journey in life and the abilities she had discovered.

She is the founder of The Return.

Olga's mission is to heal and restore femininity to its original essence.

Through Sound Reiki healing Olga is helping to shift women's inner world, restoring health, emotional stability and connection to reality, creating harmony while empowering them to return to the wisdom of their higher heart.

Olga had learned energy healing as well as the function of our minds. She had studied Rapid Transformation Therapy with Marisa Peer. That is how she learned to shift our subconscious in order to change the effects of it on our lives and health.

With her life's story Olga is recognized as a co-author of several international bestselling books and one of the leaders in healing the feminine movement.

Website:

info@thereturn.live

Social media links:

https://thereturntomyfeminineself.today

https://www.facebook.com/thereturntomyfeminineself

https://www.instagram.com/thereturntomyfeminineself

Haran Singham

CHAPTER SEVEN

Haran Singham, has been coaching professionals to discover themselves, live a meaningful and fulfilled life with purpose and have a superconscious breakthrough in their life so they can live life on their terms.

He has been coaching leaders and managers for over 15 years. As a human behavioral expert and coach, he's been working with professionals and businesses to bring out the best in them. His coaching is focused on reducing stress, increasing productivity level, team building, effective communication and relationships between employer and employees.

He coaches leaders with specific skills and tools to develop and enhance their skills. He focusses on the core skills that leaders need to manage their team as well as empowering them to be high performing teams that deliver.

Facebook Group: The Happiness Mission

Instagram: Haran.Singham

Website: www.haransingham.com

Email: haran@haransingham.com

Eve Kundycki

CHAPTER EIGHT

Intimacy coach, Architecture of the Soul, Sacred space creator

Eve is a wayfarer of the heart and soul. Her path has led her across the world and into the depths of her being. With a Master's in Architecture, Eve has a nuanced understanding of the structures necessary to build a strong foundation in both the inner and outer world.

Her journey has seen her cross oceans in a 35ft boat, train in biodynamic touch, the art of tantra, breathwork, trauma-informed coaching, and meditation. All valuable tools she now incorporates as a VITA™-certified sex, love, and relationship coach specializing in Relationship Transformation, Life Transitions, and Tantra for Couples.

Drawing from her life experiences, studies, and intuition, she now compassionately guides couples and individuals to integrate old patterns and vulnerabilities. This allows them to deepen their connection, better their communication, and expand their love in alignment with the truth of their soul. Her clients share this leads them to deeper intimacy and further along their path of self-realization.

Eve aspires to be an ambassador for kindness, authenticity, and gentle power. Often sharing her truth and the vulnerable spaces of her being, shedding light on aspects of the human condition with grace and wisdom that comes from softening and opening to life.

This chocolate-loving Belgian currently lives in Ubud, Bali, where she delights in ikebana, improv theatre, and singing.

To connect with her visit:

www.evekundycki.com

Andrea Gabriel

CHAPTER NINE

Andrea began her life in the hills of Perth, Western Australia on a beautiful 32-acre property surrounded by State Forest. She was a shy little girl who found it difficult to integrate in her early years of life. Her parents divorced when she was eight-years-old which created deep sadness and anxiety. She learned to suppress this pain with a nicotine habit from a very young age. By 14 she was homeless and couch surfing with friends and relatives until she settled in a rental property for her final year of high school.

A natural counsellor to her school peers and a very caring individual for the underprivileged and those without a voice, she embarked on study in Holistic Medicine.

She is now a registered Acupuncturist, Herbalist, Naturopath, Multi-modality therapist, Kundalini Yoga and Meditation Teacher and Women's Soft Power Empowerment Coach.

When Andrea found Kundalini Yoga and meditation, along with self-empowerment training, she was able to transform her own life and heal deep emotional wounding.

Residing in the beautiful Carmel/Bickley Valley surrounded by trees she has a stunning yoga studio and healing clinic purposely built beneath a pyramid.

It is here at Raising Vibrations Yoga Studio that she takes people on holistic healing journeys of self-discovery and love.

Her passion is to uplift and educate people to know, nurture and heal themselves. She has been a practitioner for 22 years and has a great desire for nourishing and cleansing the body with delicious wholesome food. Beyond the physical, she loves teaching people how to clear their mind of habitual thought patterns that may limit them reaching their highest potential.

www.raisingvibrationsyoga.com.au

0403189509

andreagabriel.nht@yahoo.com

Alexandra Tröstel

CHAPTER TEN

Alexandra Tröstel was born in Santiago, Chile but she resides in Sydney, Australia with her family since 1985. She lives with her daughter, a beautiful, kind, intelligent 14-year-old, a rescue dog, a recue cat; her first ever cat, and a cockatiel, so there is never a dull moment in the house.

Alexandra's work background has mainly been in Sales and Marketing but for the last three years has blossomed, starting her business journey prompted by negative situations, setting and starting up her business "Gypsy at Heart" hand carving Moais from concrete blocks and creating woodwork pieces to decorate the home and garden.

Alexandra tries to dedicate as much time as she can to music. She loves to play guitar and sing as often as she can, and has written her own original songs, having recorded one, with more to come!

Loves supporting live bands and shows as often as she can.

She lives life in a positive way, believes in Karma and in treating others how we want to be treated. Alexandra loves to surround herself with her loving family and a genuine circle of friends!

Alexandra's life philosophy is to "Love big, hold tightly, laugh from the core of your stomach, dance like no one is watching, don't just sing in the shower, compromise and fight for love and forgive where you can!, not when you're expected to."

You can follow Alexandra on her music channel Alexandra Music: https://youtube.com/watch?v=3sjVygOnOCU&feature=share

And her Instagram account "Gypsy at Heart": gypsy_at_heart_2020

John Spender

CHAPTER ELEVEN

John Spender is a 30-time International Best Selling co-author, who didn't learn how to read and write at a basic level until he was ten-years-old. He has since traveled to more than 65 countries, territories and started many businesses leading him to create the best-selling book series *A Journey Of Riches*. He is an Award Winning International Speaker and Movie Maker.

John worked as an international NLP trainer and coached thousands of people from various backgrounds through many challenges. From the borderline homeless to wealthy individuals, he has helped many people connect with their truth to create a life on their terms.

John's search for answers to living a fulfilling life has taken him to work with Native American Indians in the Hills of San Diego, to the forests of Madagascar, swimming with humpback whales in Tonga, exploring the Okavango Delta of Botswana and climbing the Great Wall of China. He's traveled from Chile to Slovakia, Hungary to the Solomon Islands, the mountains of Italy and the streets of Mexico.

Everywhere his journey has taken him, John has discovered a hunger among people to find a new way to live, with a yearning for freedom of expression. His belief that everyone has a book in them was born.

He is now a writing coach, having worked with over 400 authors from 40 countries for the *A Journey of Riches* series http://ajourneyofriches.com/ and his publishing house, Motion Media International, has published 31 non-fiction titles to date.

John also wrote and produced the movie documentary *Adversity* starring Jack Canfield, Rev. Micheal Bernard Beckwith, Dr. John Demartini and many more, coming soon in 2022. And you can bet there will be a best-selling book to follow!

ACKNOWLEDGMENTS

Reading and writing are gifts that very few give to themselves. It is such a powerful way to reflect and gain closure from the past; reading and writing are therapeutic processes. The experience raises one's self-esteem, confidence, and awareness of self.

I learned this when I collated the first book in the *A Journey of Riches* series, which now includes thirty-one books with over 300 co-authors from over forty different countries. It's difficult to write about your personal experiences, and I honor and respect every author who has collaborated in the series.

For many authors, English is their second language, which is a significant achievement. In creating this anthology of short stories, I have been touched by the generosity, gratitude, and shared energy this experience has given everyone.

The inspiration for *A Journey of Riches, Master Your Mindset* was born from my desire to share insights about how changing your mindset change everything in your life. Each chapter is written by a different author sharing their wisdom on mastering their mindset to create a more fulfilling life.

I want to thank all the authors for entrusting me with their unique memories, encounters, and wisdom. Thank you for sharing and opening the door to your soul so others may learn from your experience. I trust the readers will gain confidence from your successes and wisdom from your failures.

I also want to thank my family. I know you are proud of me, seeing how far I have come from that ten-year-old boy learning how to read and write at a basic level. Big shout out to my Mom, Robert, Dad, Merril; my brother Adam and his daughter Krystal; my sister Hollie, her partner Brian, my nephew Charlie and niece, Heidi;

thank you for your support. Also, kudos to my grandparents, Gran, and Pop, who are alive and well, and Ma and Pa, who now rest in peace. They accept me just the way I am with all my travels and adventures around the world.

Thanks to the team at Motion Media International; you have done an excellent job at editing and collating this book. It was a pleasure working with you on this successful project, and I thank you for your patience in dealing with the changes and adjustments along the way.

Thank you, the reader, for having the courage to look at your life and how you can improve your future in a fast and rapidly changing world.

Thank you again to my fellow co-authors: Amanda Lees, Dr. Olga Zabora, PsyD, Bec Bucci, Kyle Zagrodzky, Olga Brooks, Alexandra Tröstel, Haran Singham, Andrea Gabriel, Eve Kundycki, and Inarra Aryane Griffyn.

With gratitude,
John Spender

Afterword

I hope you enjoyed the collection of heartfelt stories, wisdom and vulnerability shared. Storytelling is the oldest form of communication, and I hope you feel inspired to take a step toward living a fulfilling life. Feel free to contact any of the authors in this book or the other books in this series.

The proceeds of this book will feed many of the rural Balinese families that are struggling.

Other books in the series are…

Transform Your Wounds into Wisdom: A Journey of Riches, Book Thirty
https://mybook.to/WoundsintoWisdom

Motivate Your Life: A Journey of Riches, Book Twenty Nine
https://www.amazon.com/dp/B0BCXMF11P

Awaken to Your Inner Truth: A Journey of Riches, Book Twenty Eight
https://www.amazon.com/dp/B09YLYMQ4H?geniuslink=true

The Power of Inspiration: A Journey of Riches, Book Twenty Seven
http://mybook.to/ThePowerofInspiration

Messages from The Heart: A Journey of Riches, Book Twenty Six
http://mybook.to/MessagesOfHeart

Abundant living: A Journey of Riches, Book Twenty Five
https://www.amazon.com/dp/B0963N6B2C

The Way of the Leader: A Journey of Riches, Book Twenty Four
https://www.amazon.com/dp/1925919285

The Attitude of Gratitude: A Journey of Riches, Book Twenty Three
https://www.amazon.com/dp/1925919269

Facing your Fears: A Journey of Riches, Book Twenty Two
https://www.amazon.com/dp/1925919218

Returning to Love: A Journey of Riches, Book Twenty One
https://www.amazon.com/dp/B08C54M2RB

Develop Inner Strength: A Journey of Riches, Book Twenty
https://www.amazon.com/dp/1925919153

Building your Dreams: A Journey of Riches, Book Nineteen
https://www.amazon.com/dp/B081KZCN5R

Liberate your Struggles: A Journey of Riches, Book Eighteen
https://www.amazon.com/dp/1925919099

In Search of Happiness: A Journey of Riches, Book Seventeen
https://www.amazon.com/dp/B07R8HMP3K

Tapping into Courage: A Journey of Riches, Book Sixteen
https://www.amazon.com/dp/B07NDCY1KY

The Power Healing: A Journey of Riches, Book Fifteen
https://www.amazon.com/dp/B07LGRJQ2S

The Way of the Entrepreneur: A Journey Of Riches, Book Fourteen
https://www.amazon.com/dp/B07KNHYR8V

Discovering Love and Gratitude: A Journey Of Riches, Book Thirteen
https://www.amazon.com/dp/B07H23Q6D1

Transformational Change: A Journey Of Riches, Book Twelve
https://www.amazon.com/dp/B07FYHMQRS

Finding Inspiration: A Journey Of Riches, Book Eleven
https://www.amazon.com/dp/B07F1LS1ZW

Building your Life from Rock Bottom: A Journey Of Riches, Book Ten
https://www.amazon.com/dp/B07CZK155Z

Transformation Calling: A Journey Of Riches, Book Nine
https://www.amazon.com/dp/B07BWQY9FB

Letting Go and Embracing the New: A Journey Of Riches, Book Eight
https://www.amazon.com/dp/B079ZKT2C2

Making Empowering Choices: A Journey Of Riches, Book Seven
https://www.amazon.com/Making-Empowering-Choices-Journey-Riches-ebook/dp/B078JXMK5V

The Benefit of Challenge: A Journey Of Riches, Book Six
https://www.amazon.com/dp/B0778S2VBD

Personal Changes: A Journey Of Riches, Book Five
https://www.amazon.com/dp/B075WCQM4N

Dealing with Changes in Life: A Journey Of Riches, Book Four
https://www.amazon.com/dp/B0716RDKK7

Making Changes: A Journey Of Riches, Book Three
https://www.amazon.com/dp/B01MYWNI5A

The Gift In Challenge: A Journey Of Riches, Book Two
https://www.amazon.com/dp/B01GBEML4G

From Darkness into the Light: A Journey Of Riches, Book One
https://www.amazon.com/dp/B018QMPHJW

Thank you to all the authors who have shared aspects of their lives, hoping to inspire others to live a bigger version of themselves.

I want to share a beautiful quote from the great Jim Rohan, "You can't complain and feel grateful at the same time." At any given moment, we have a choice to either feel like a victim of life or be connected and grateful for it. I hope this book helps you feel grateful and inspires you to go after your dreams.

For more information about contributing to the series, visit http://ajourneyofriches.com/. Furthermore, if you enjoyed reading this book, we would appreciate your review on Amazon to help get our message out to even more readers.

Made in the USA
Monee, IL
26 February 2023

28335698R00116